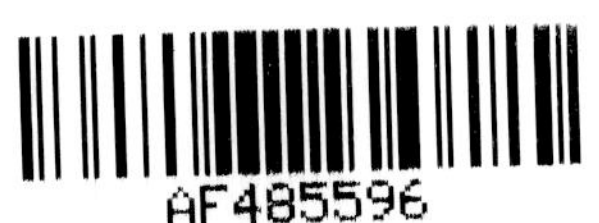

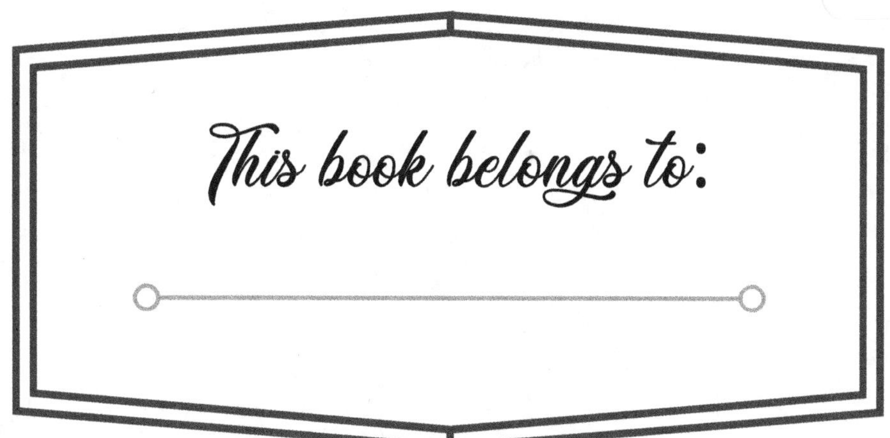

COLORFUL FLOWER DESIGNS

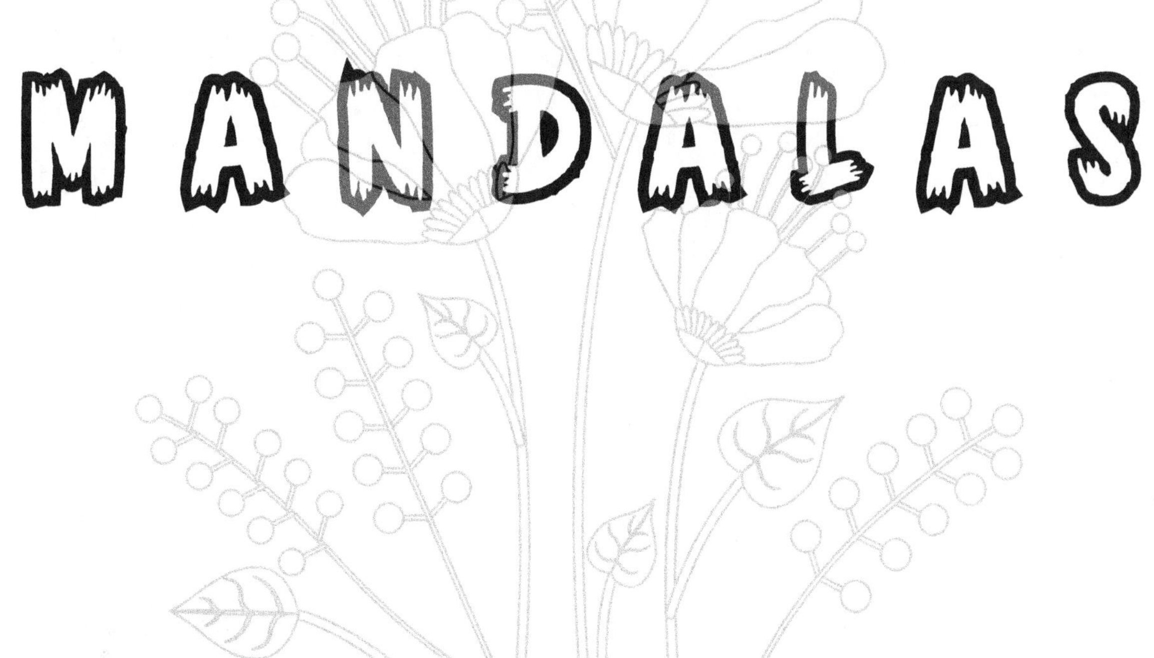

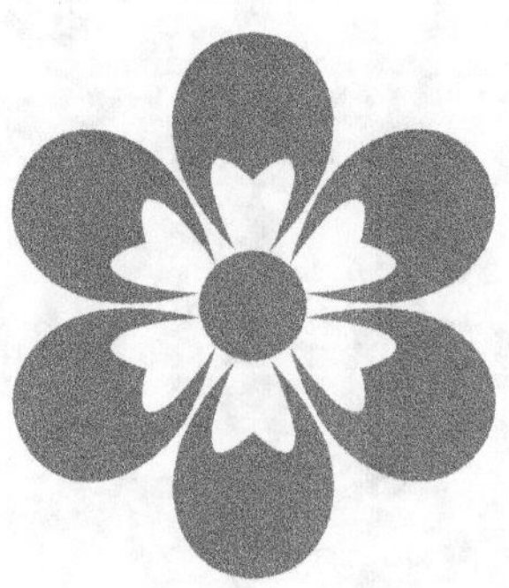

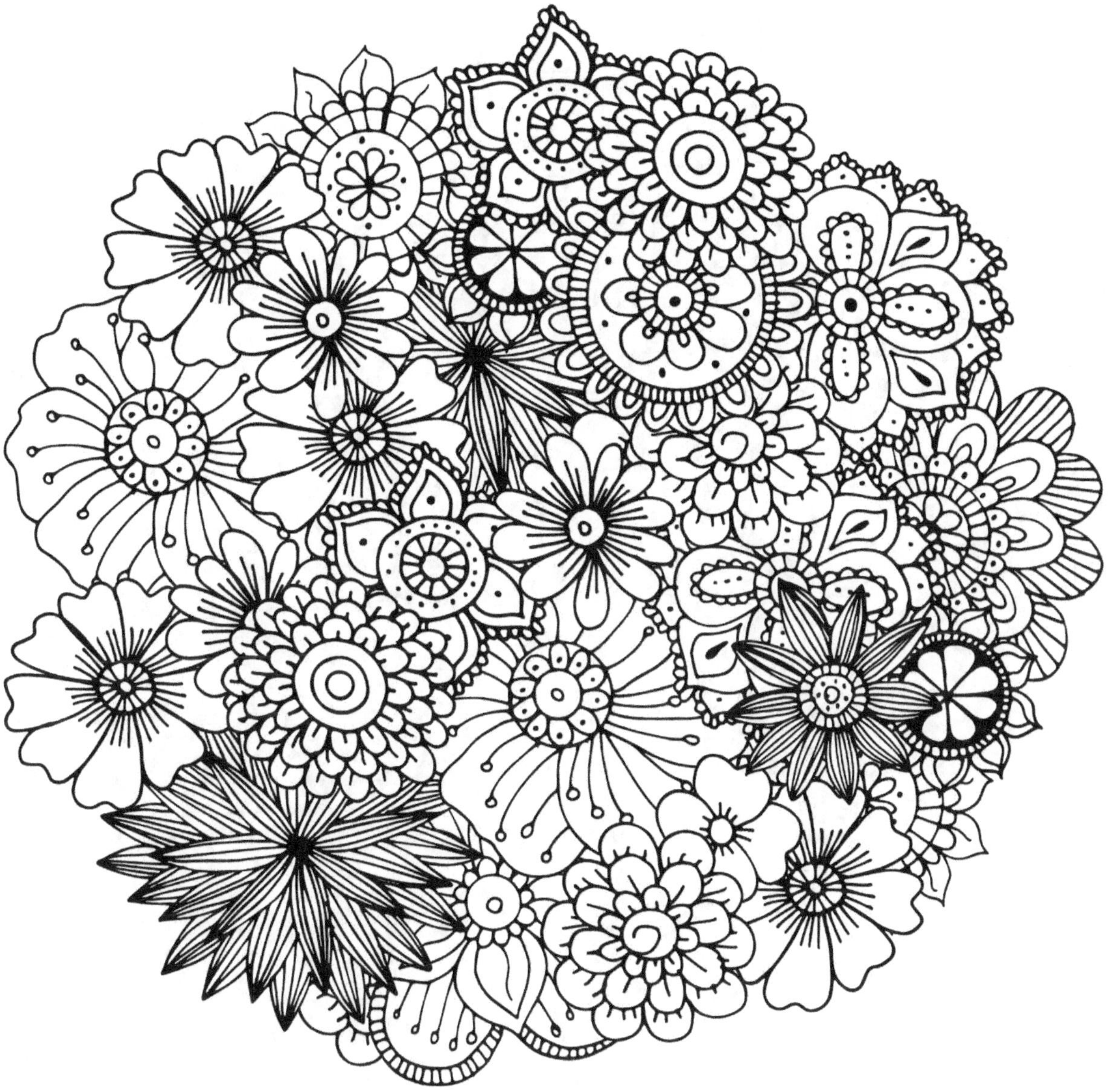

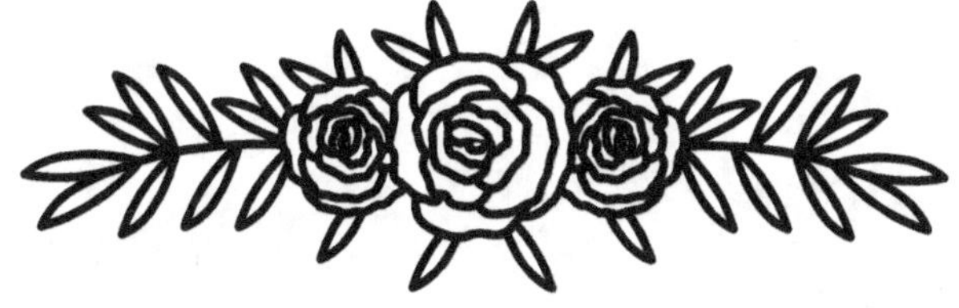

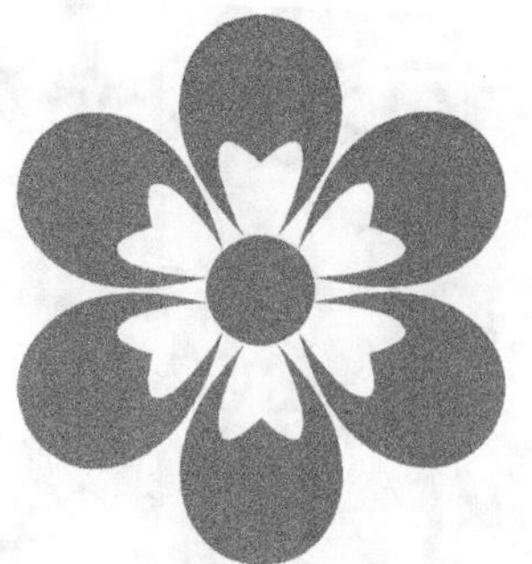

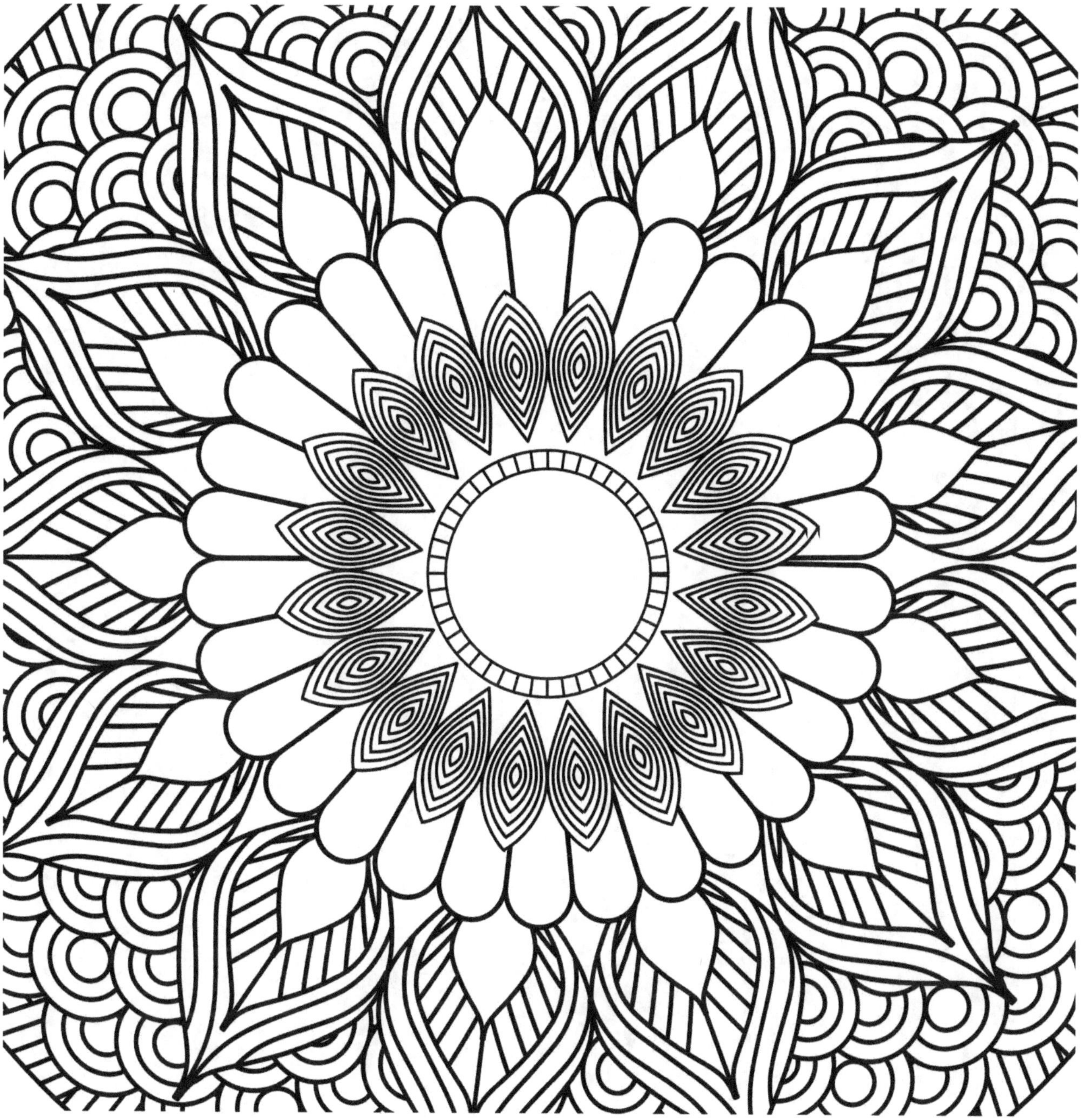

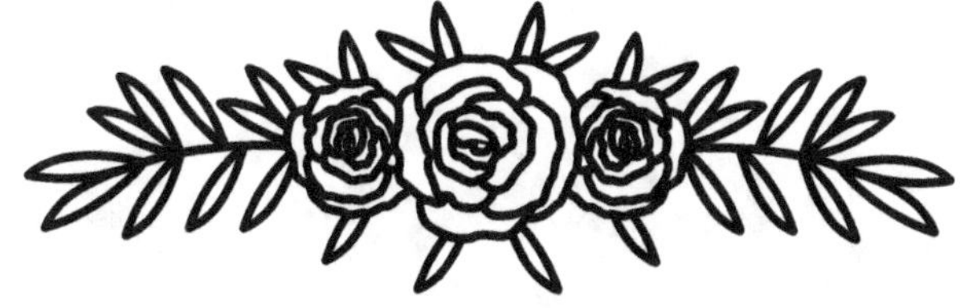

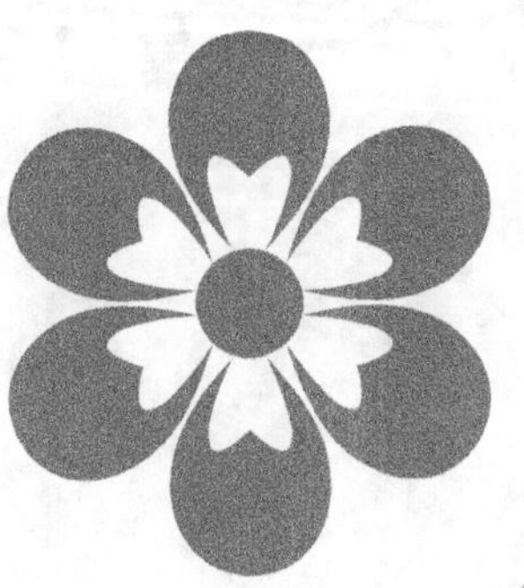

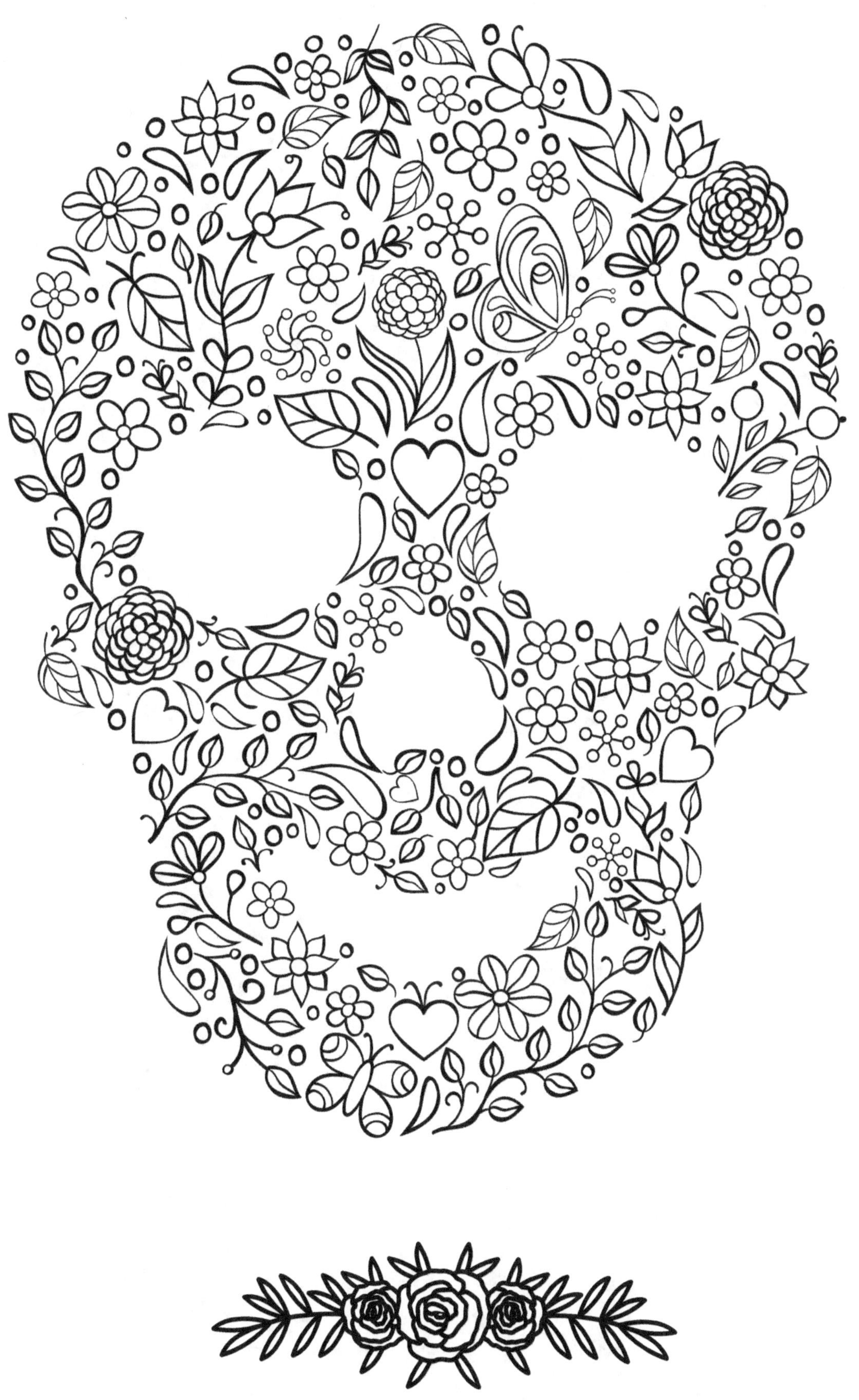

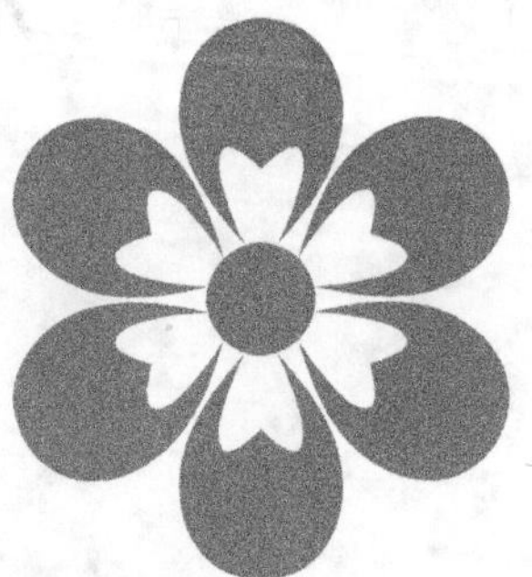

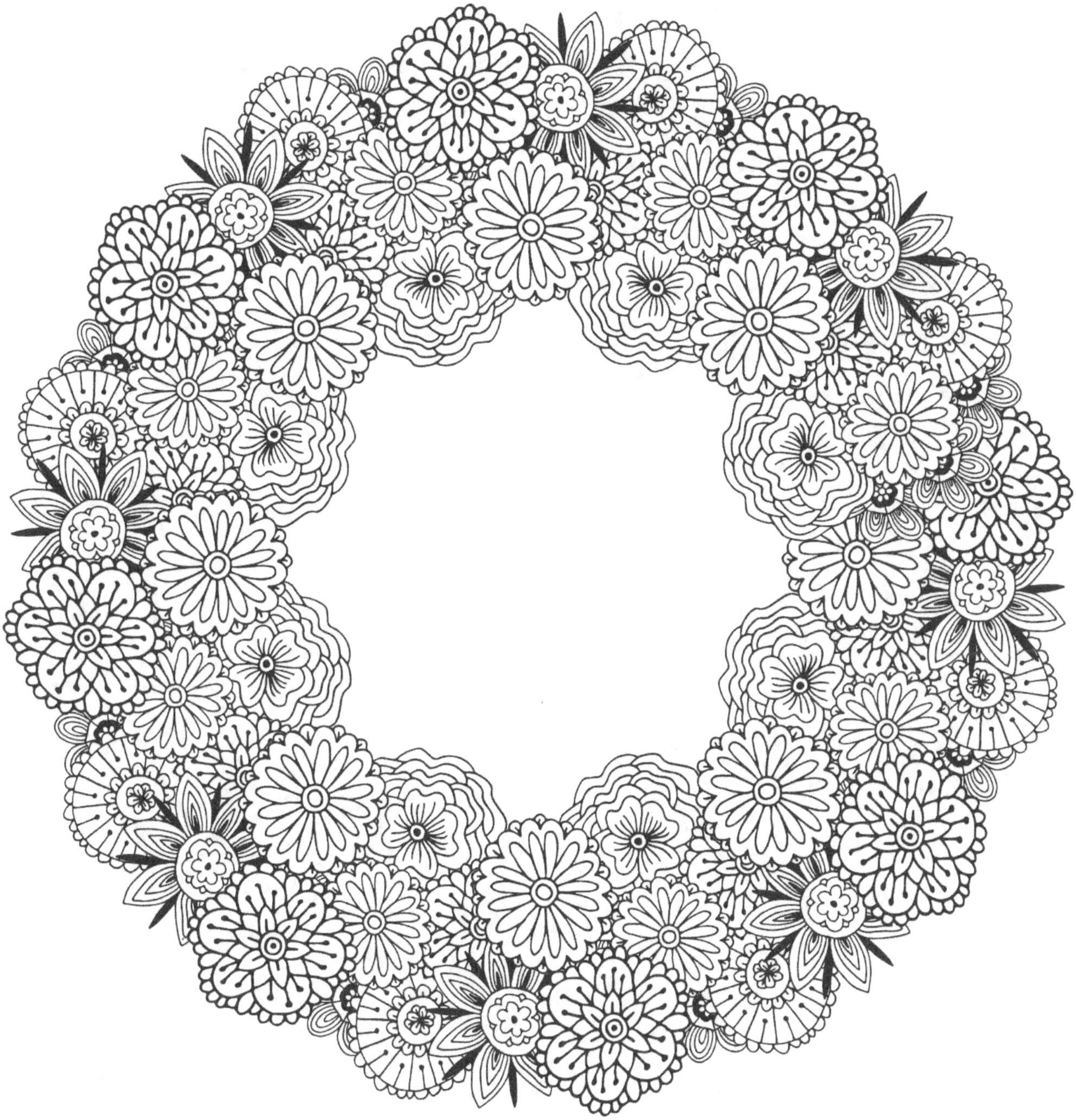

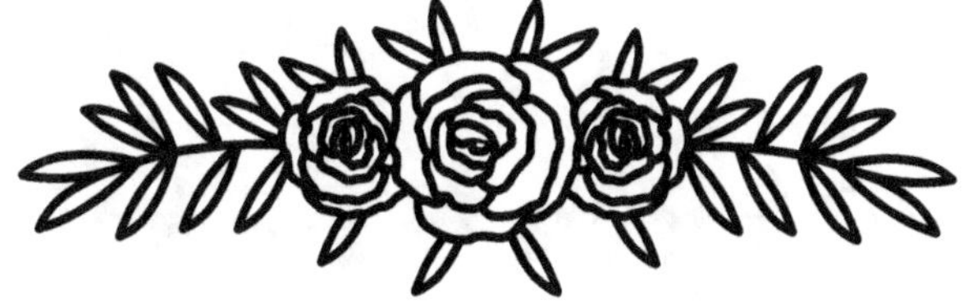

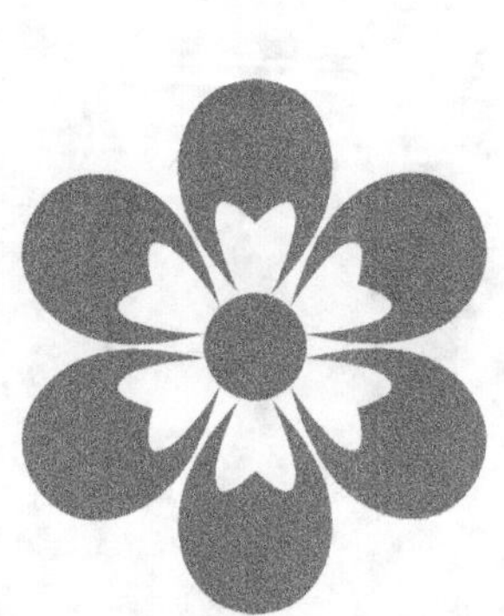

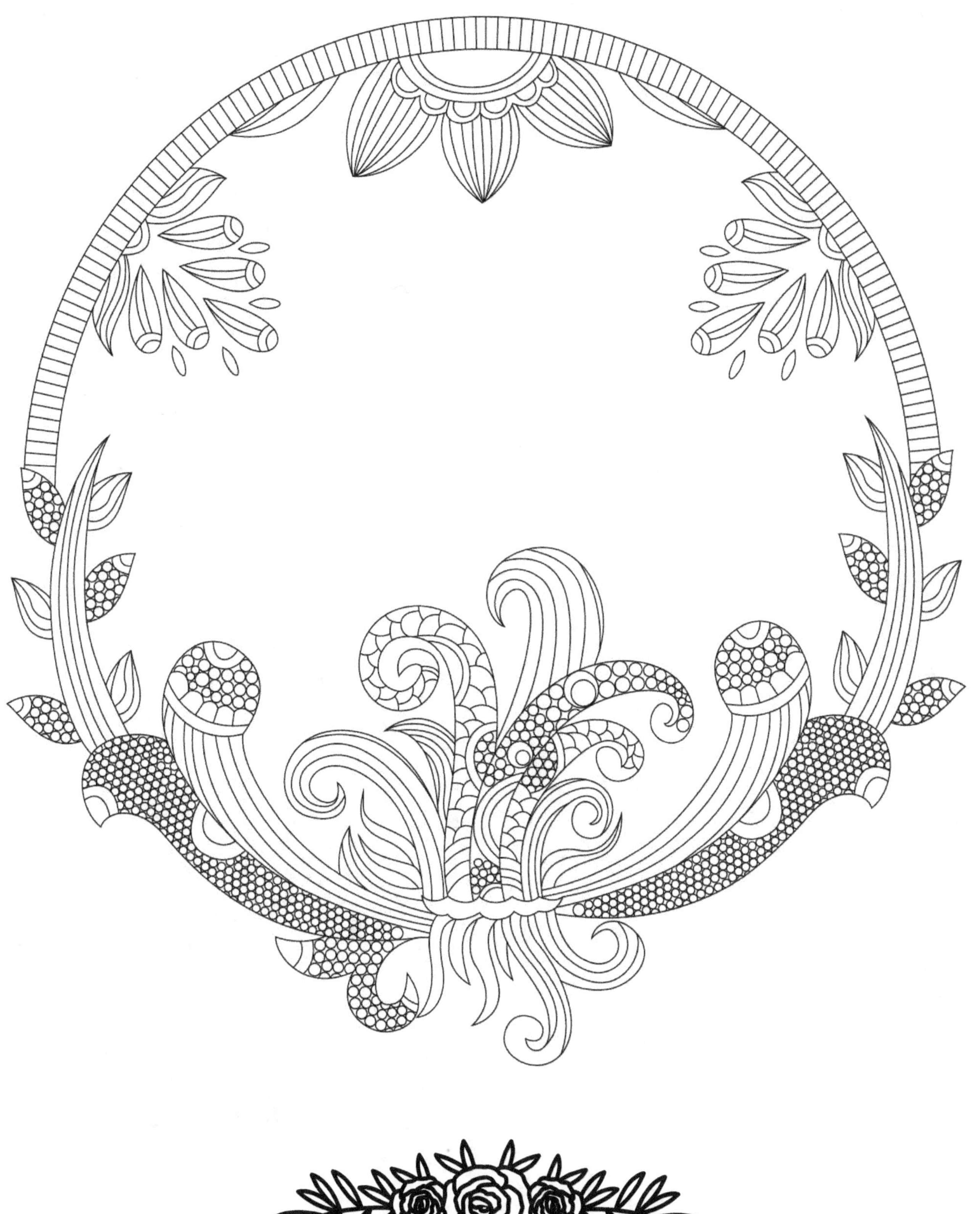

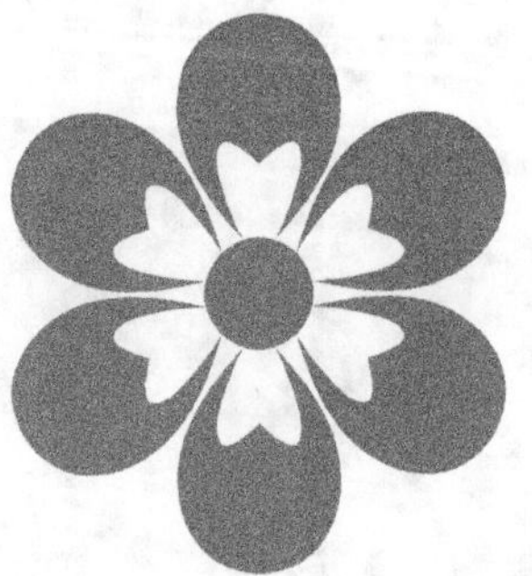

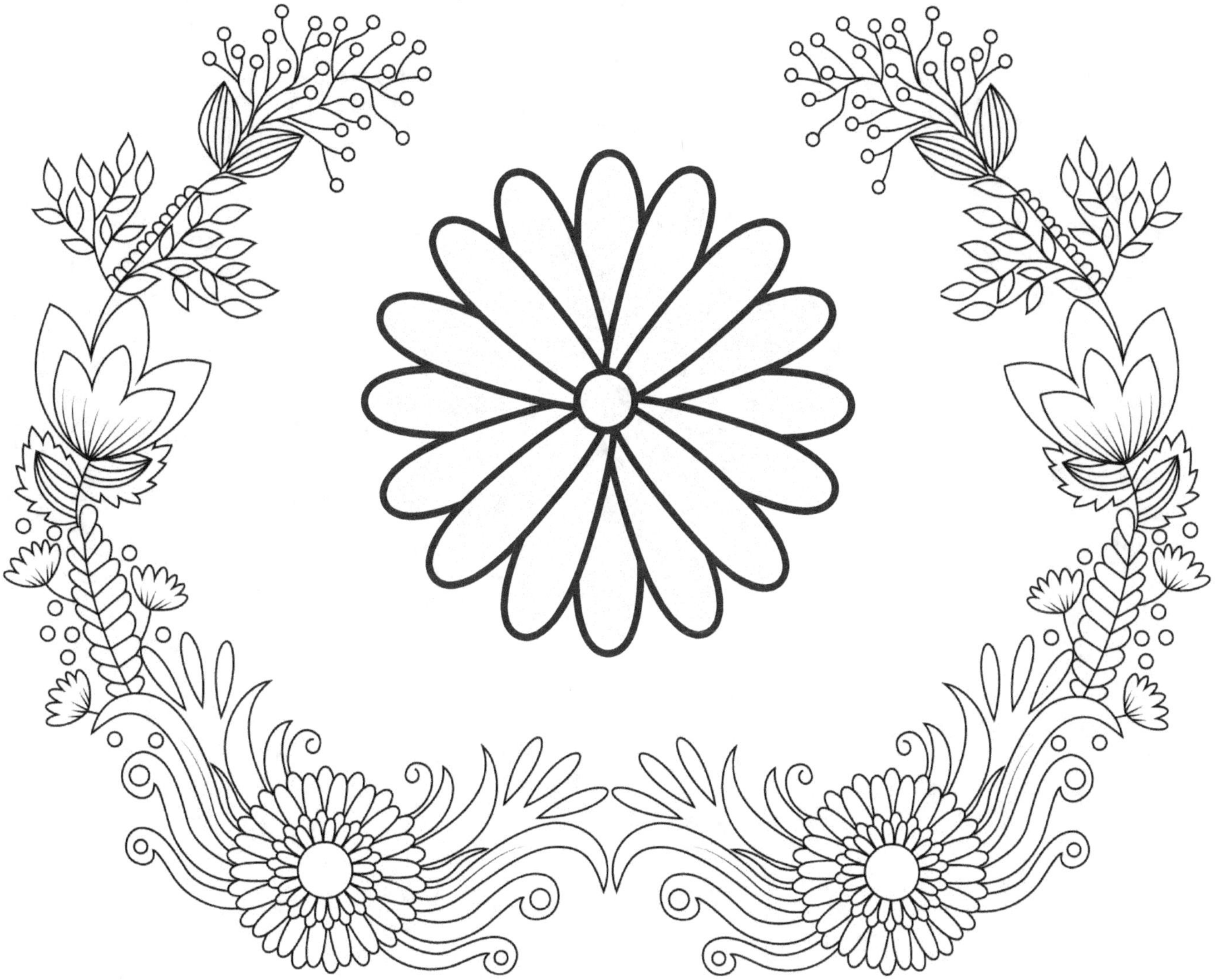

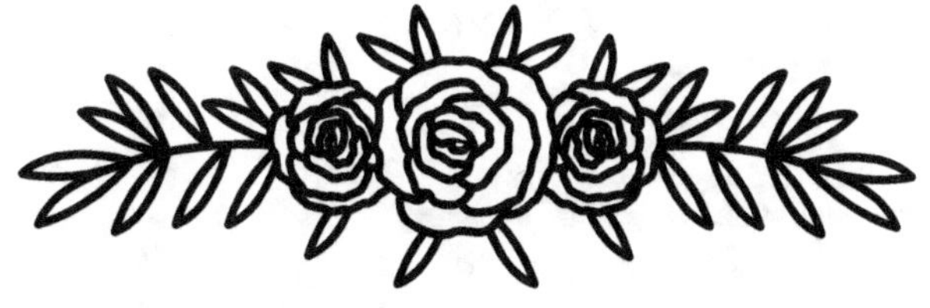

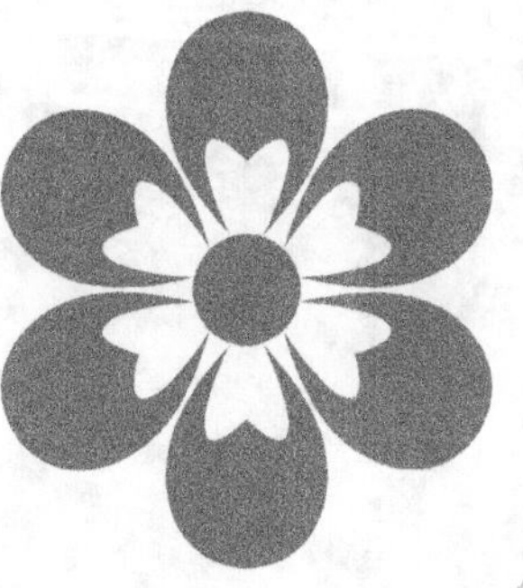

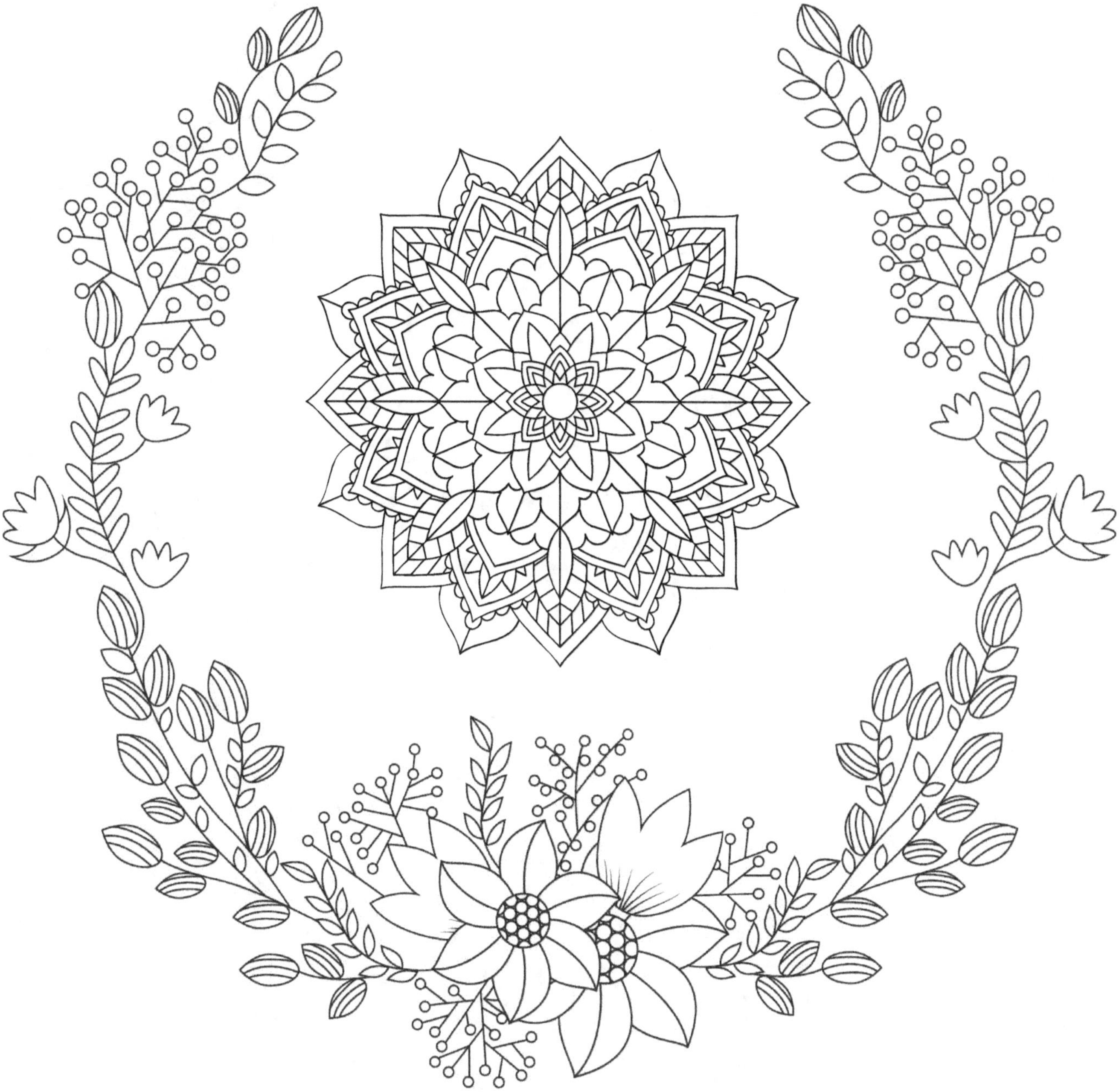

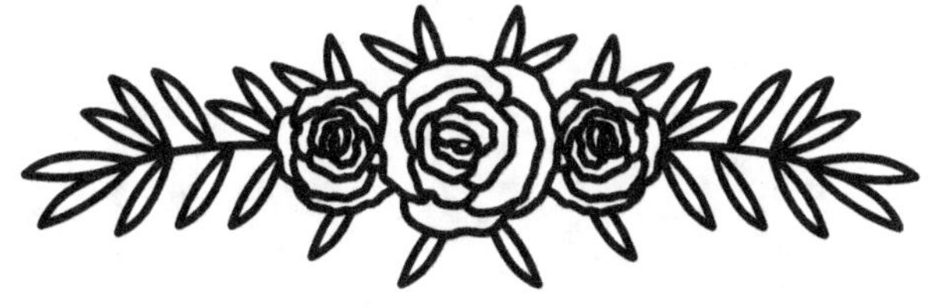

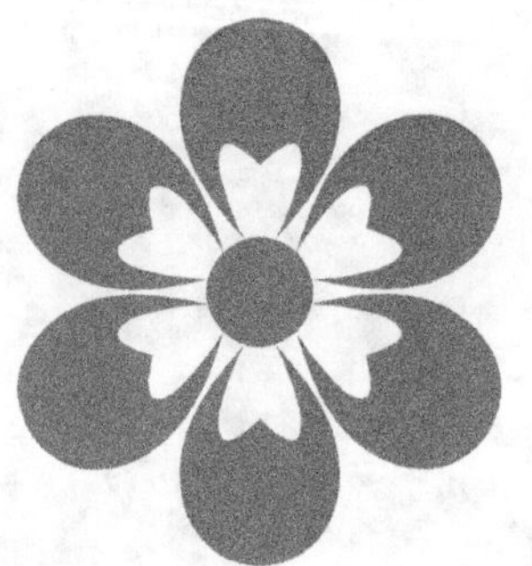

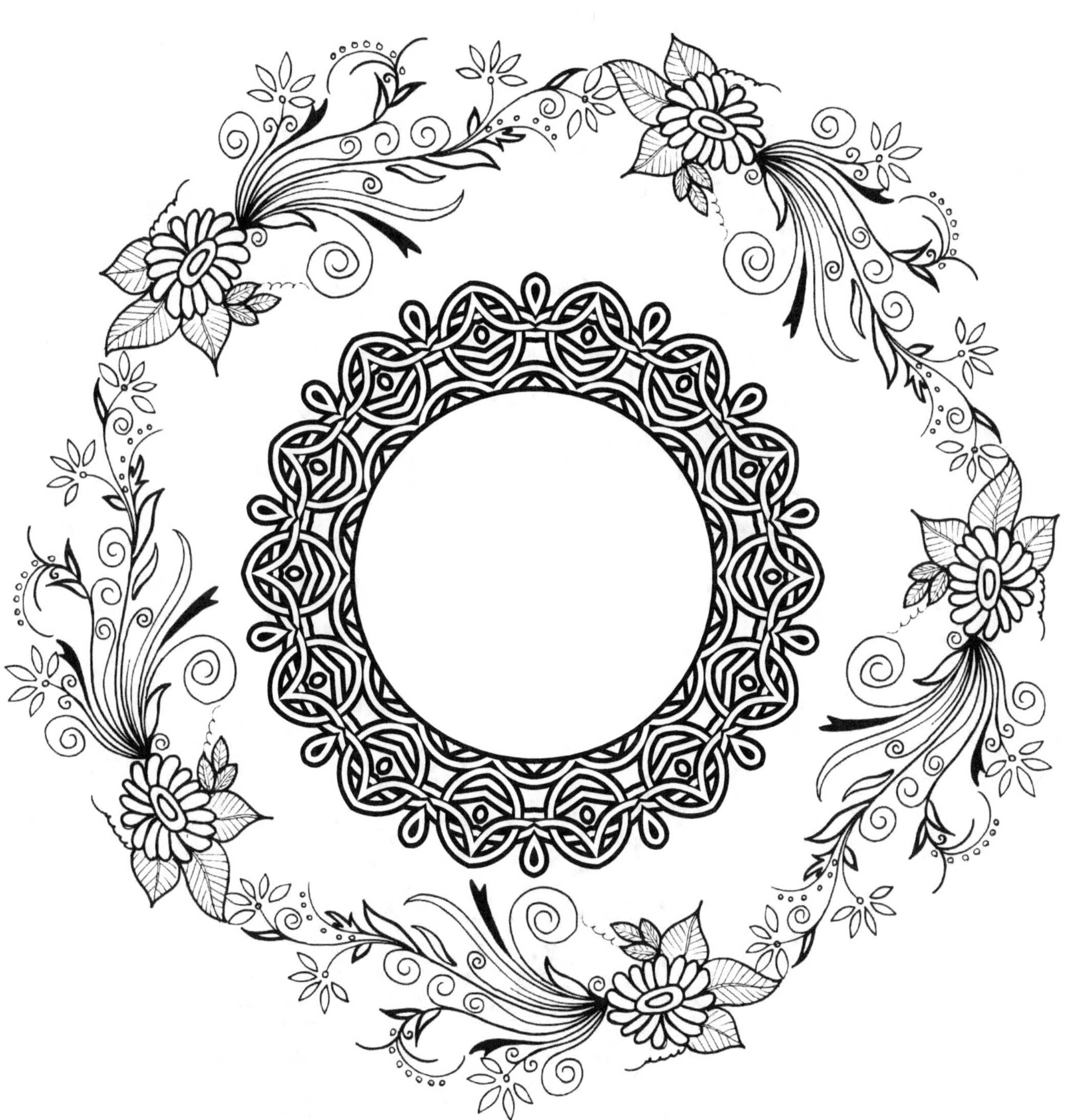

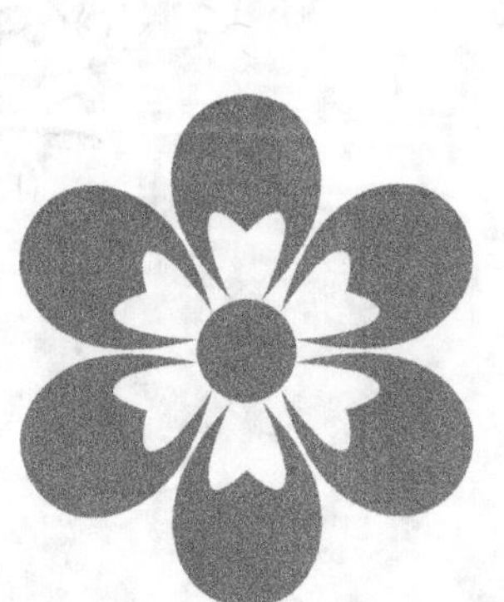

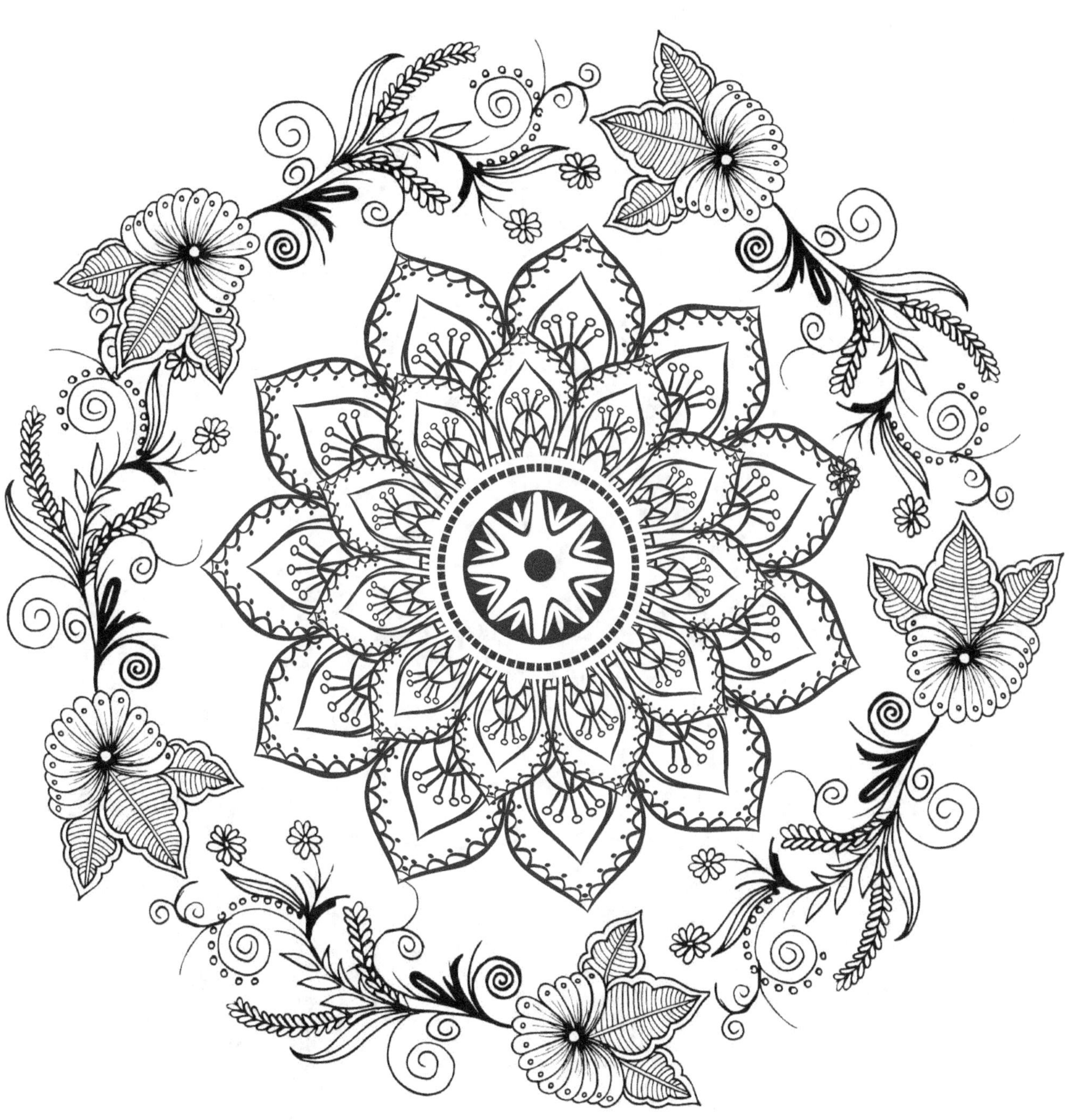

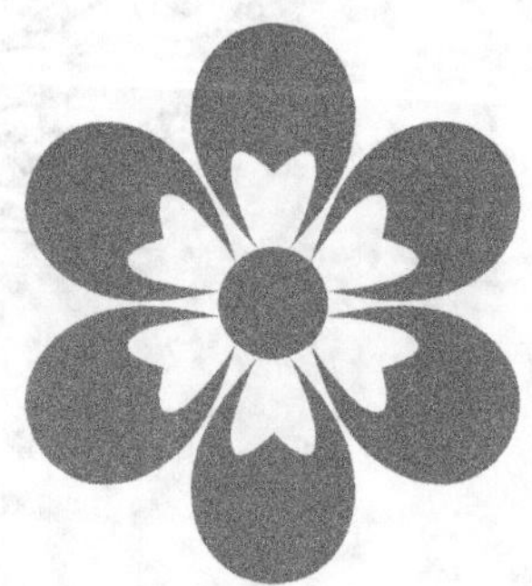

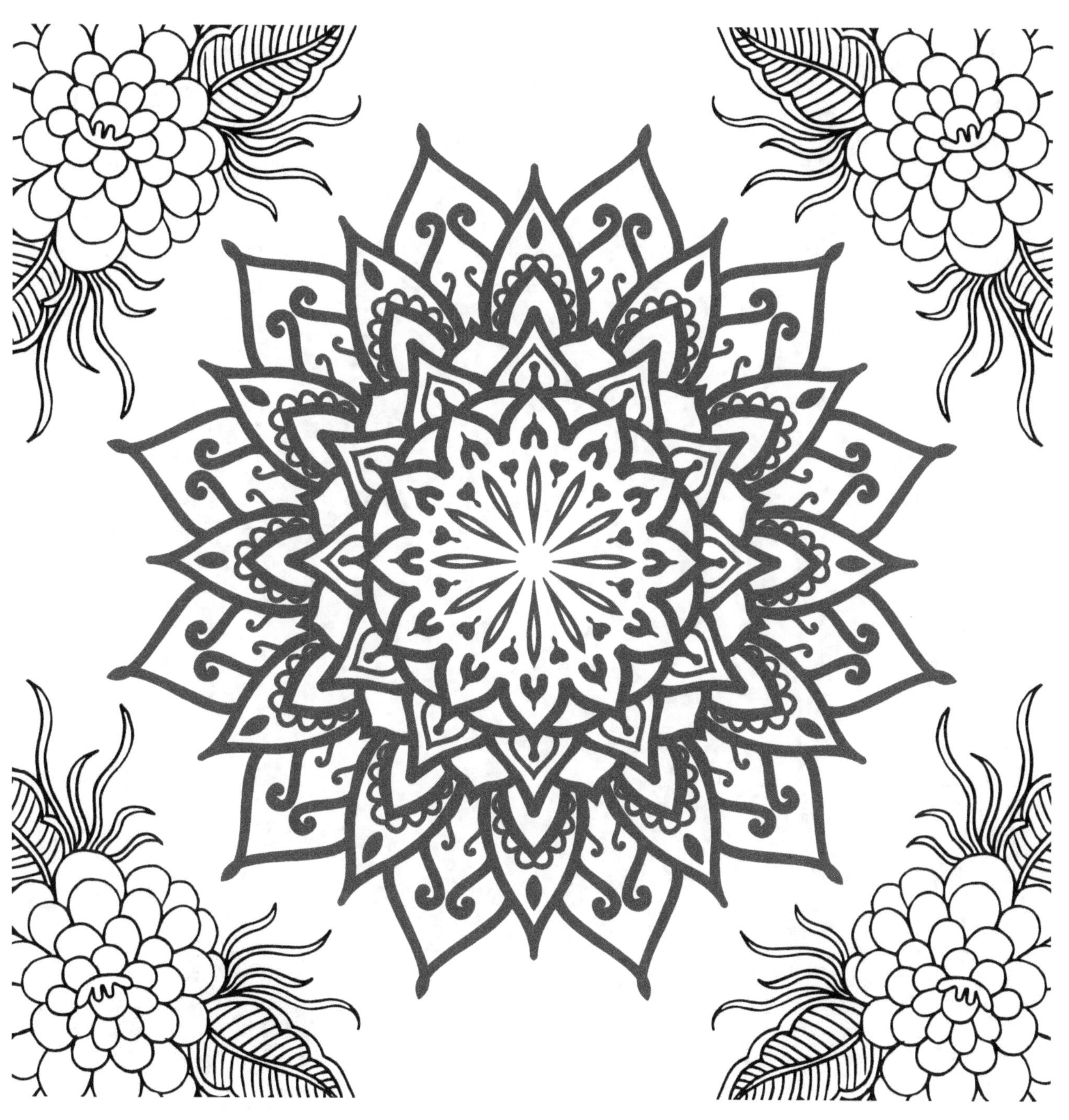

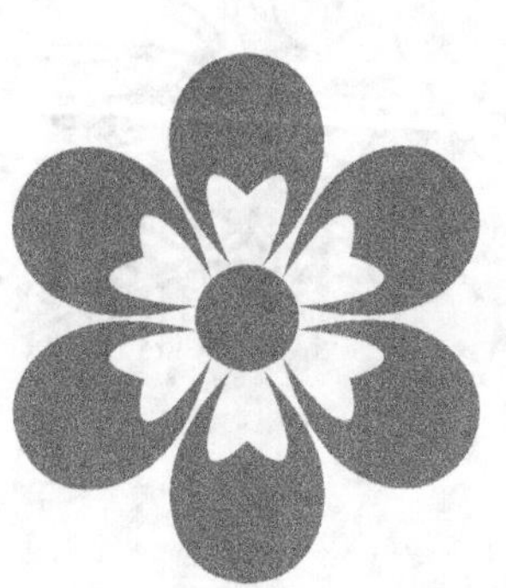

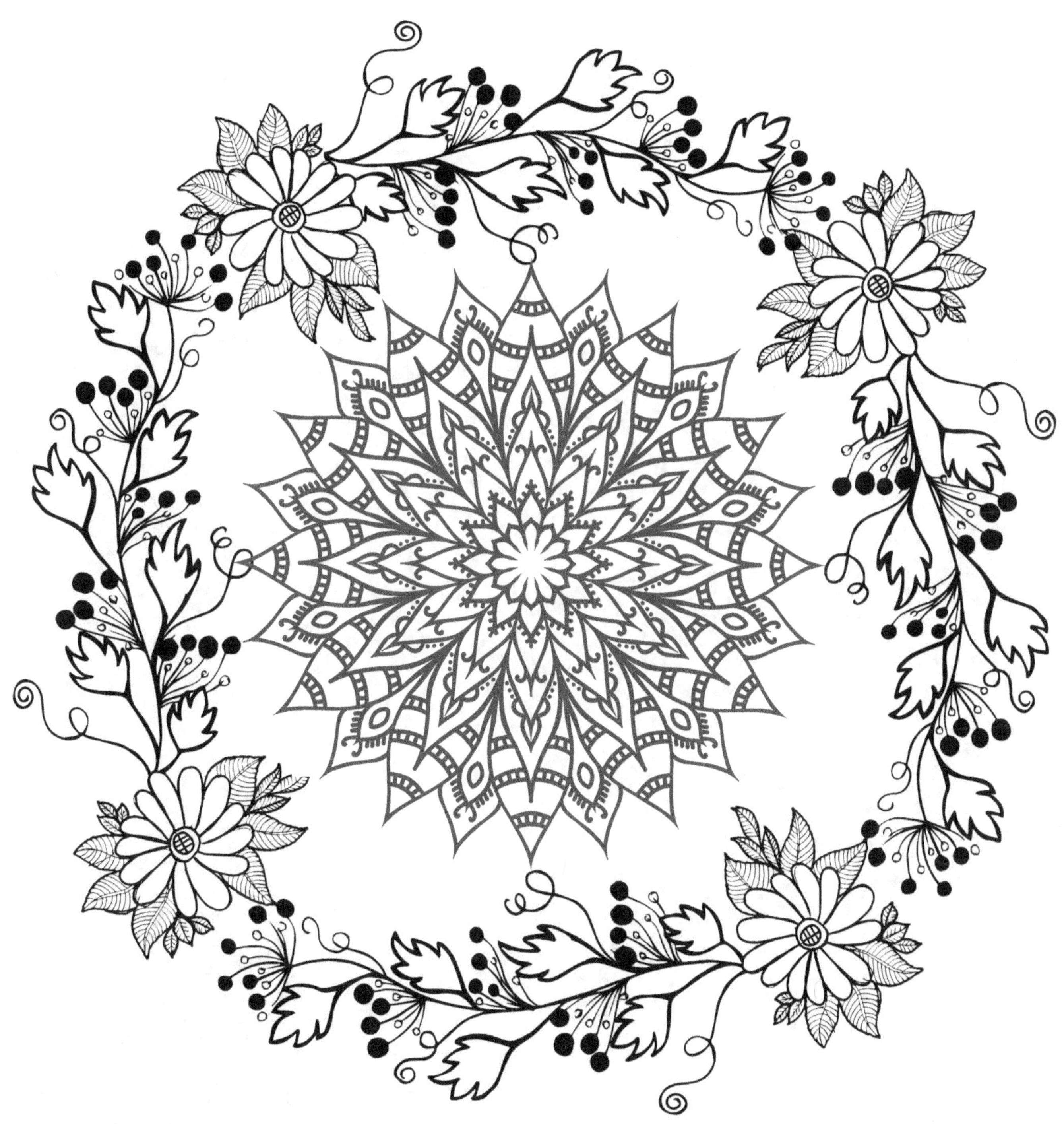

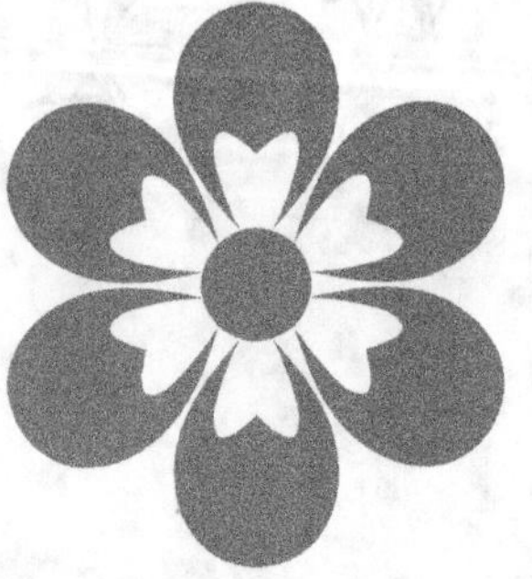

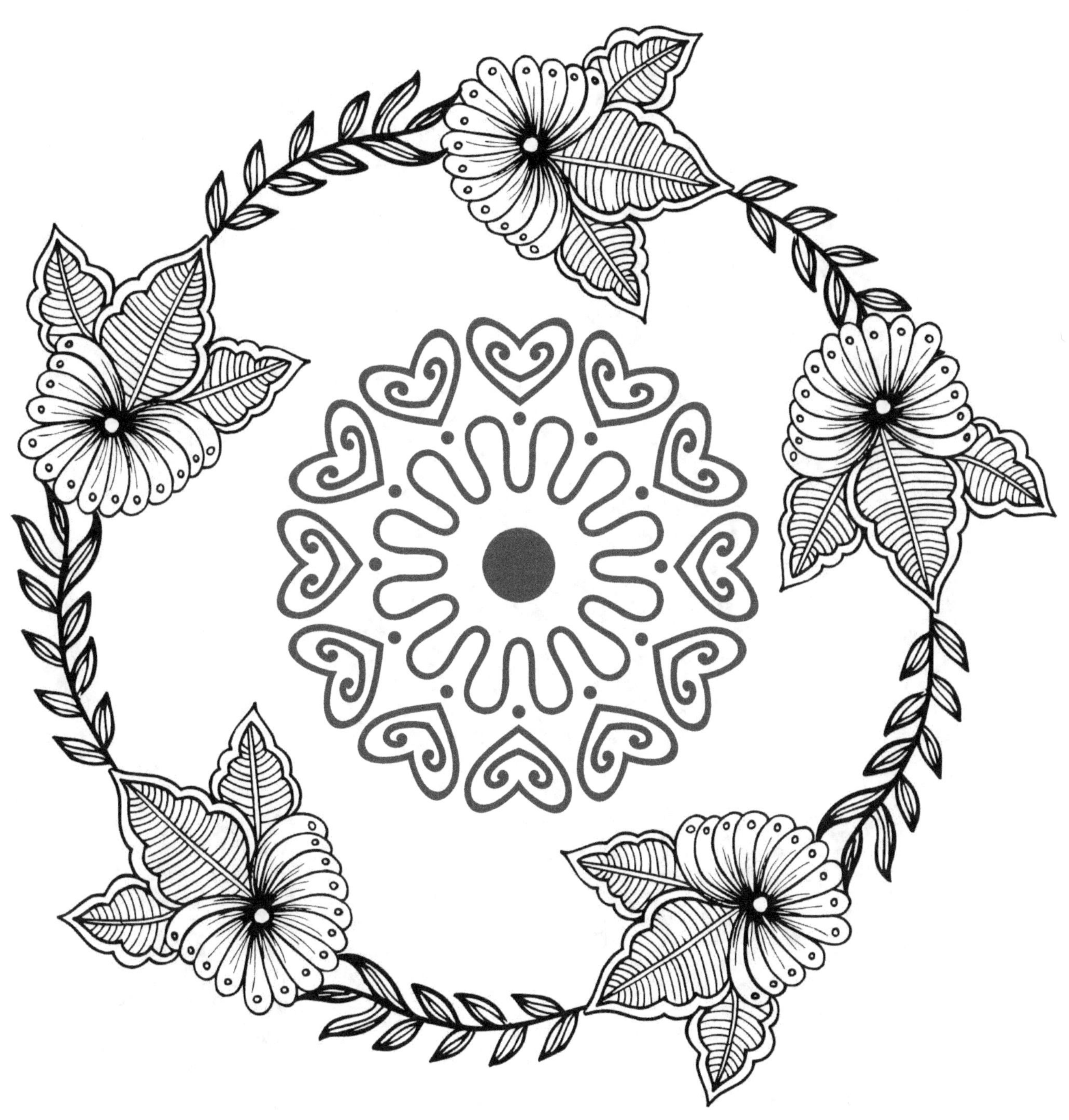

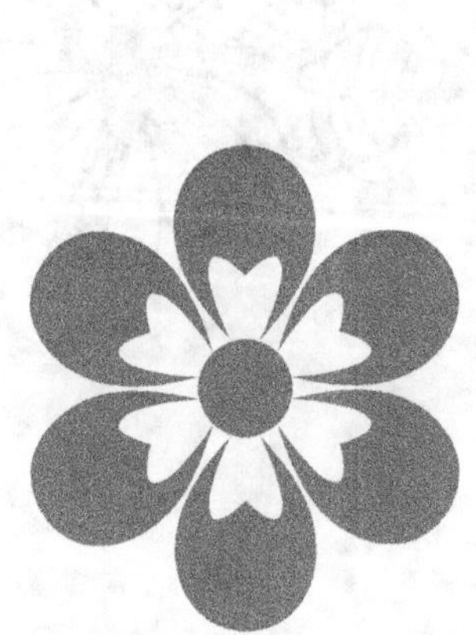

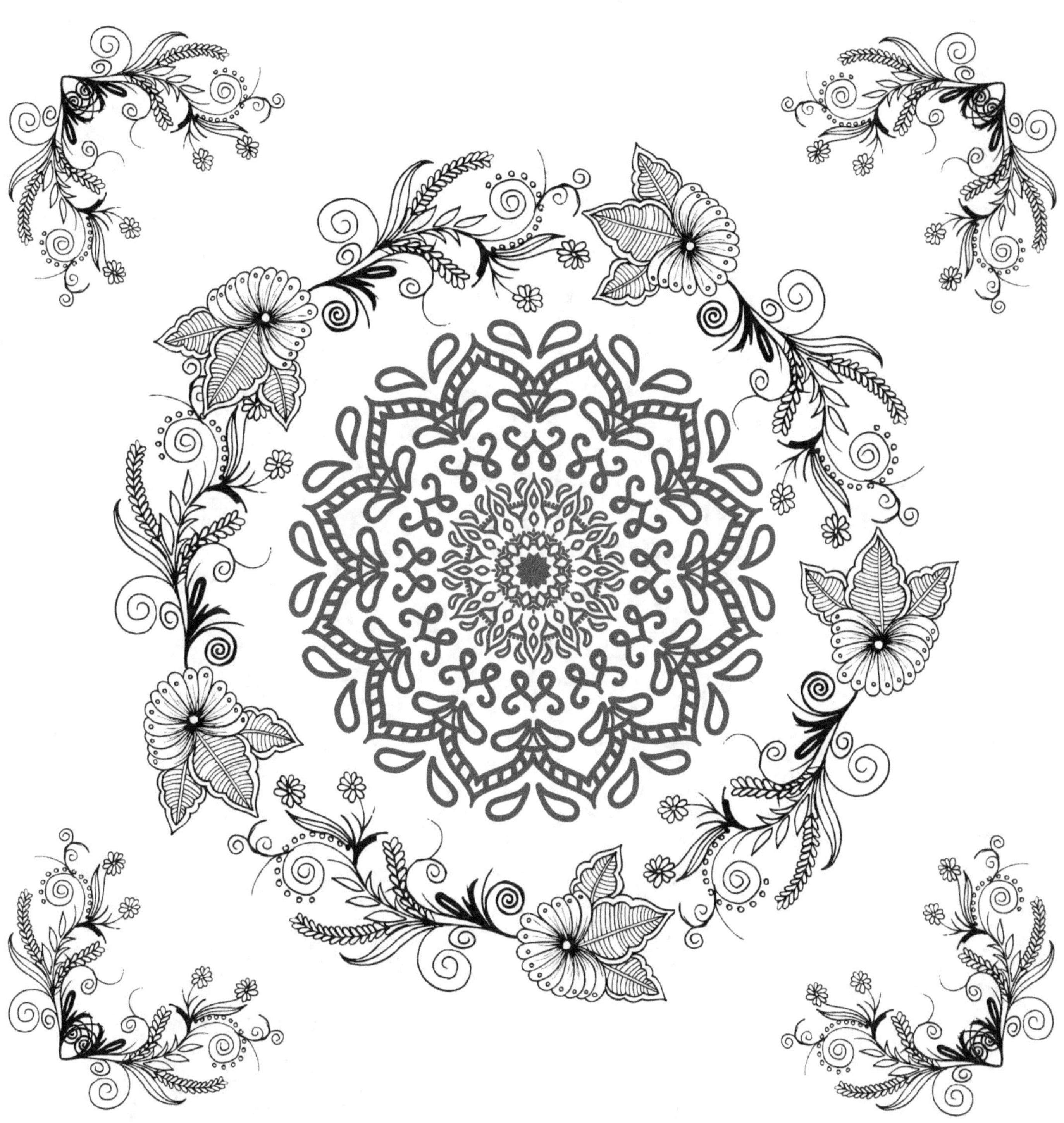

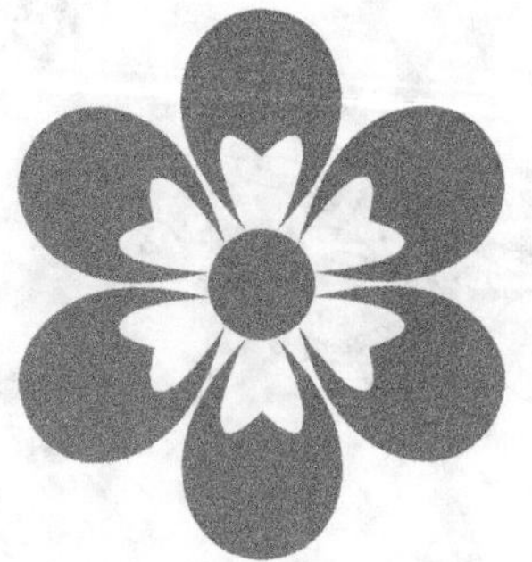

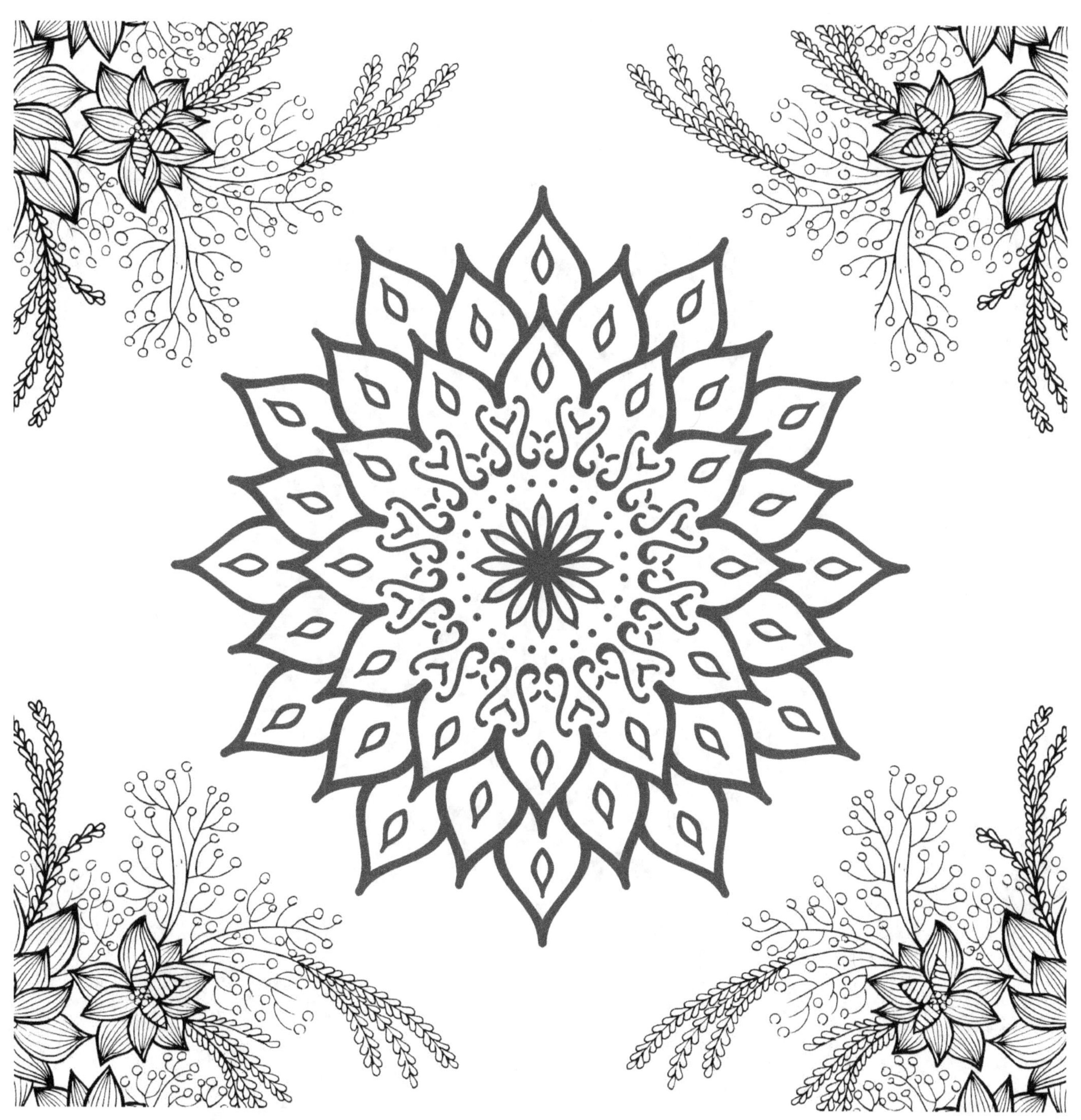

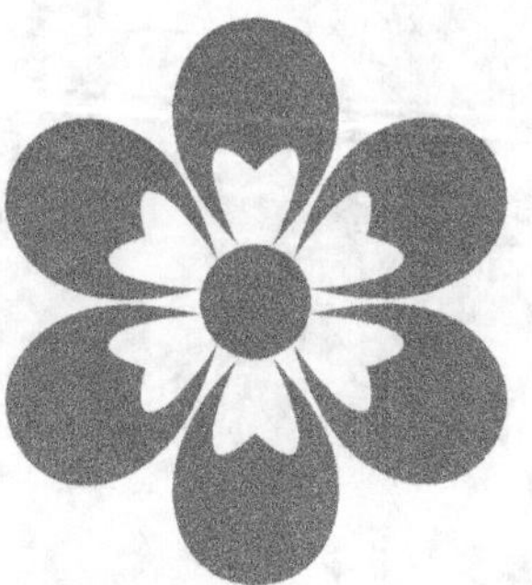

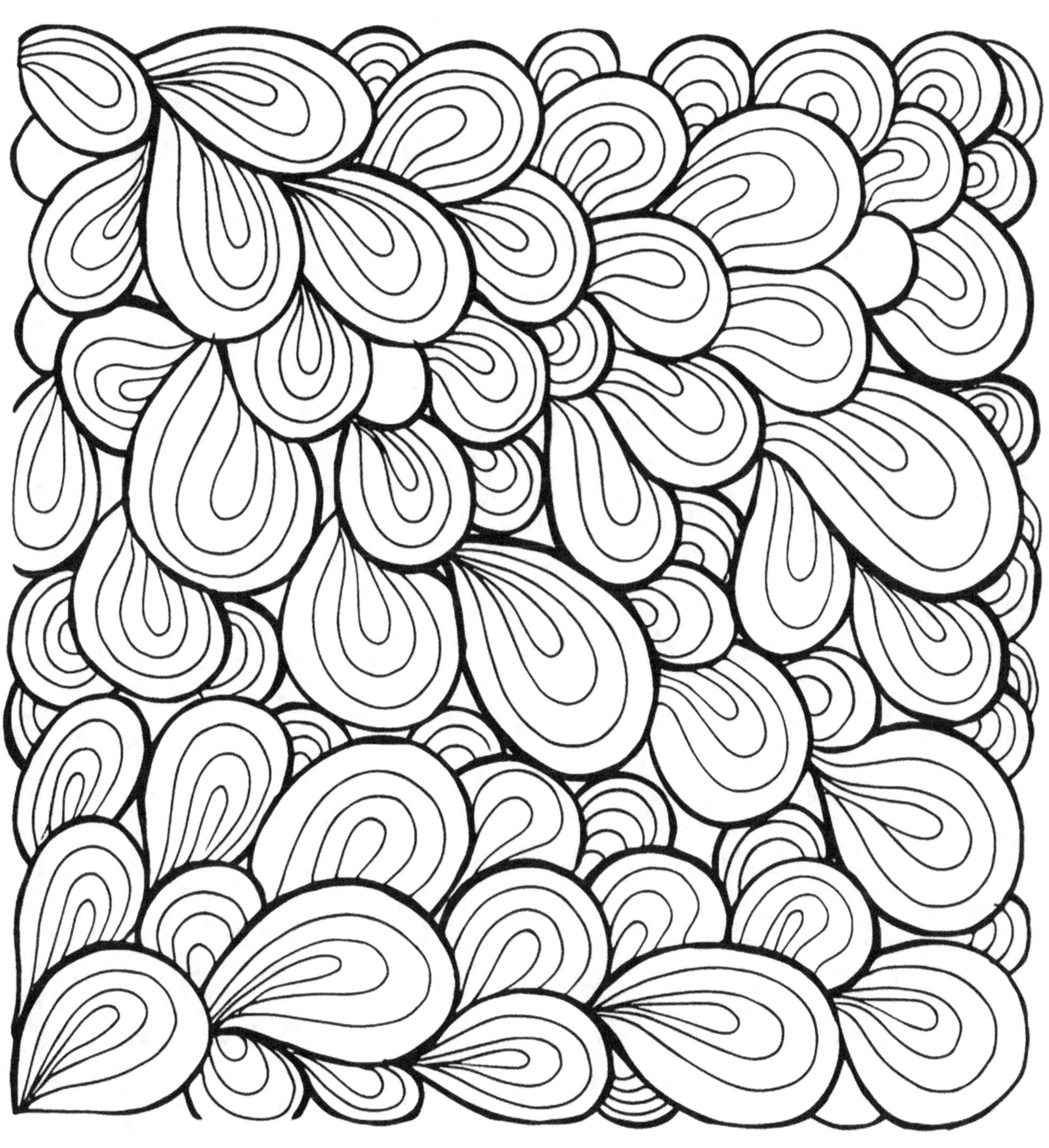

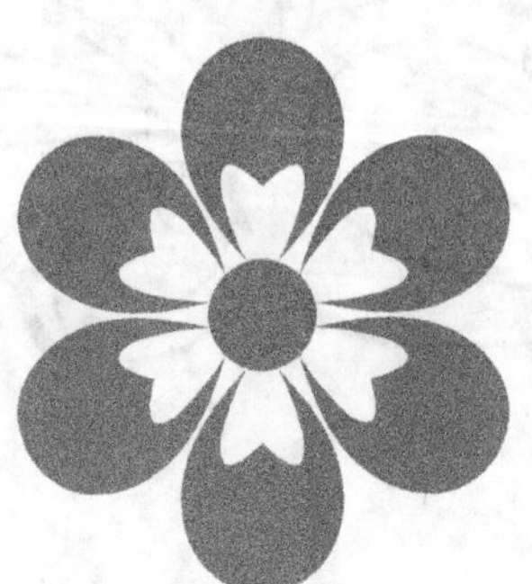

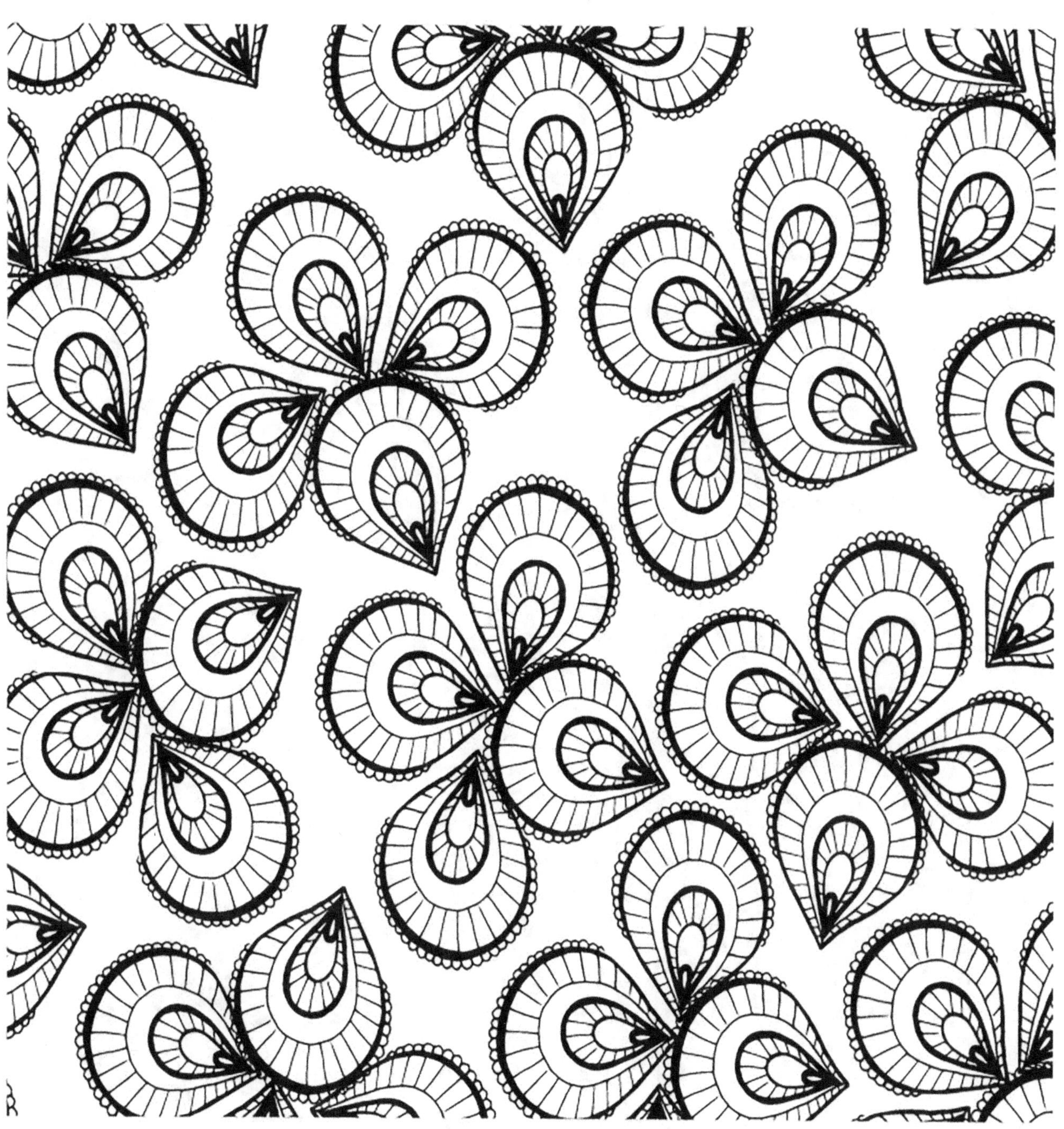

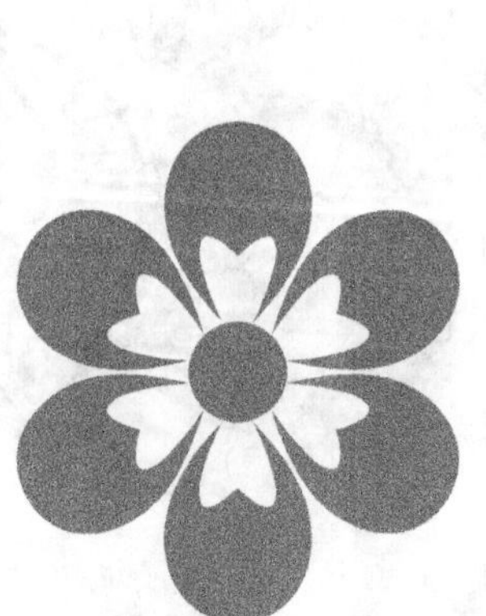

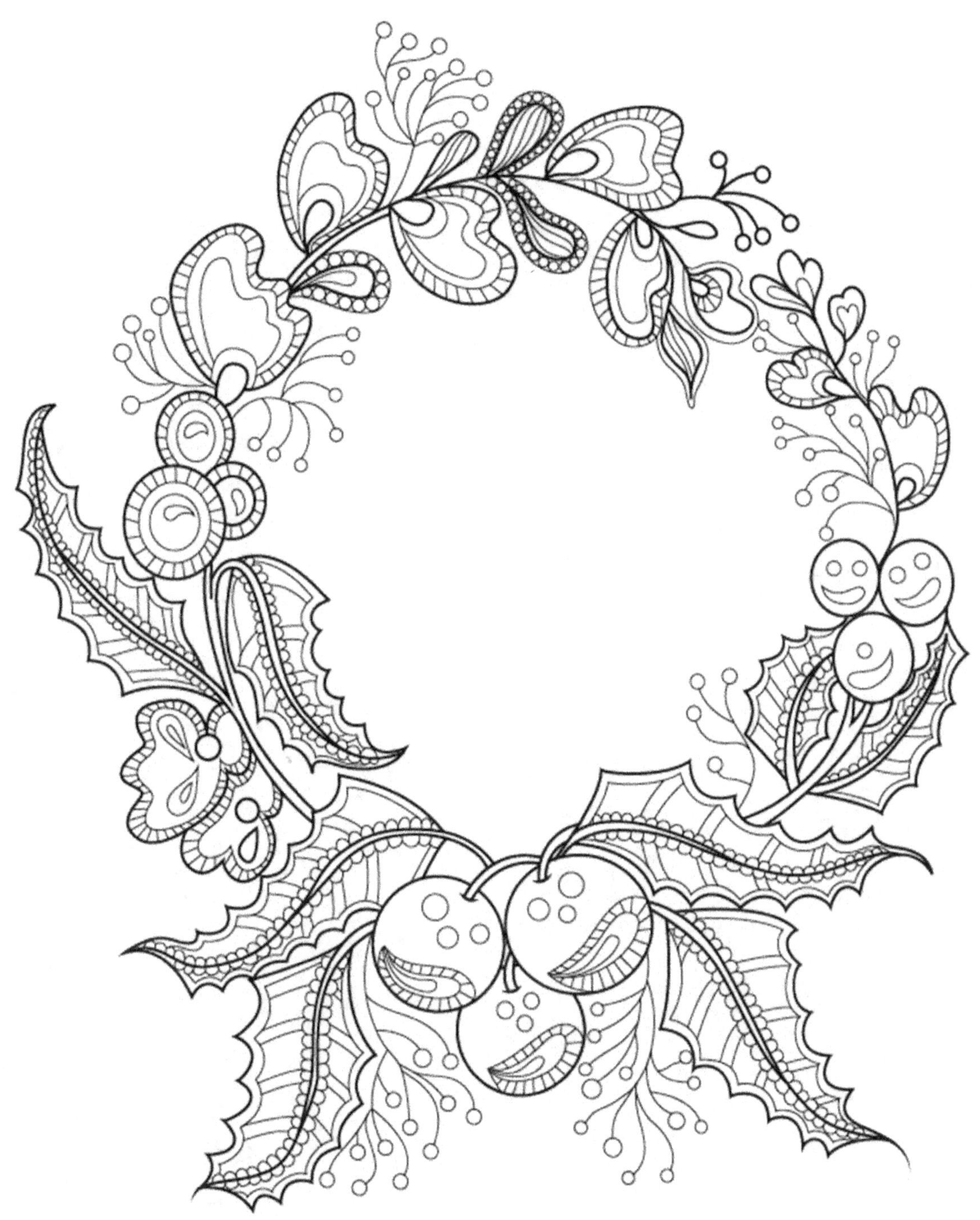

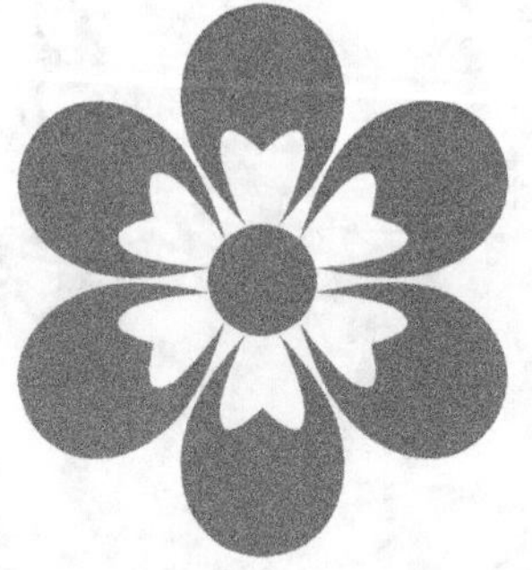

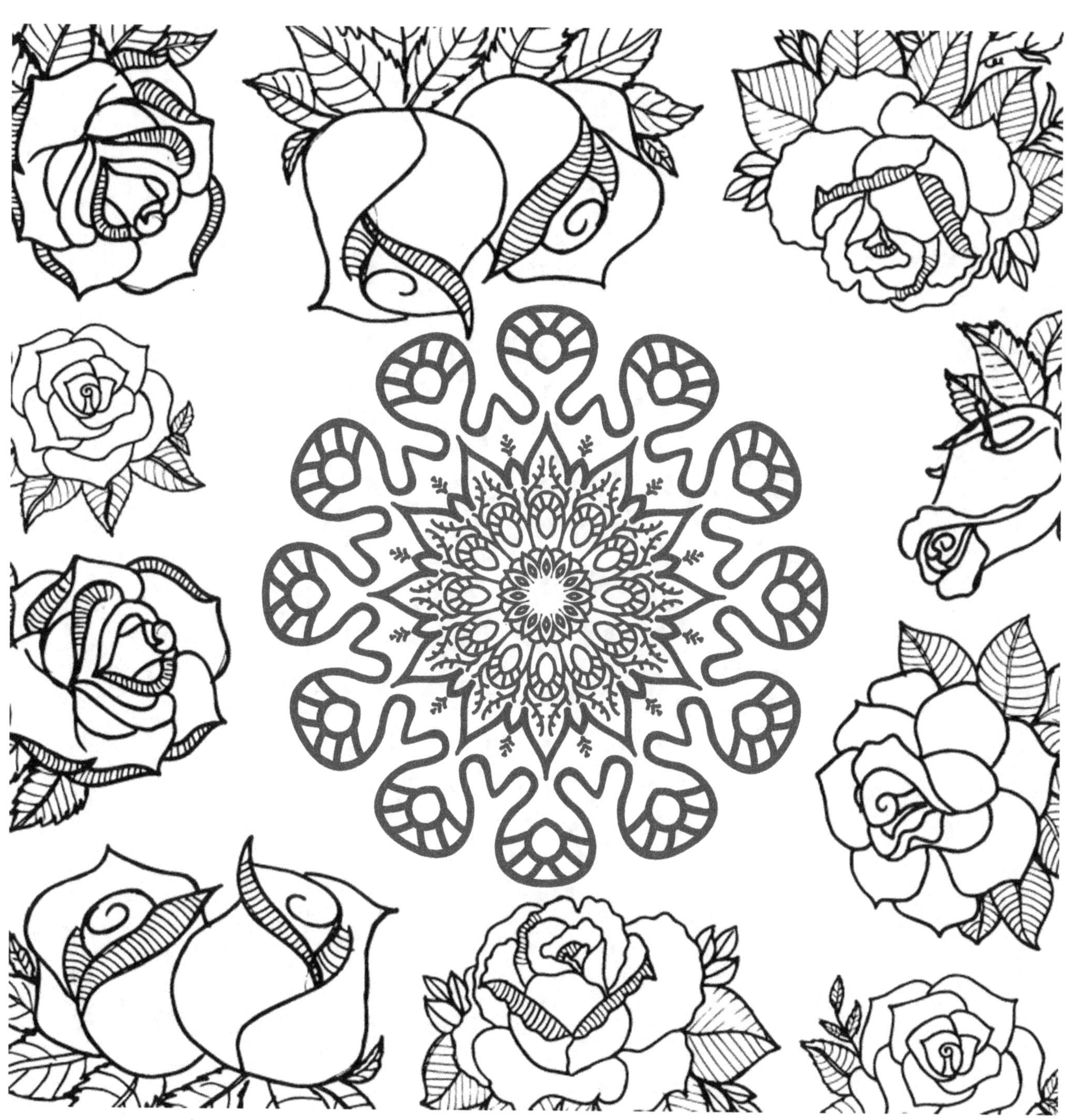

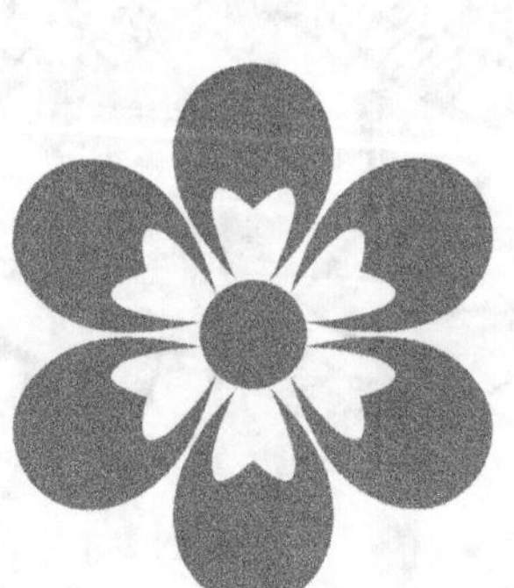

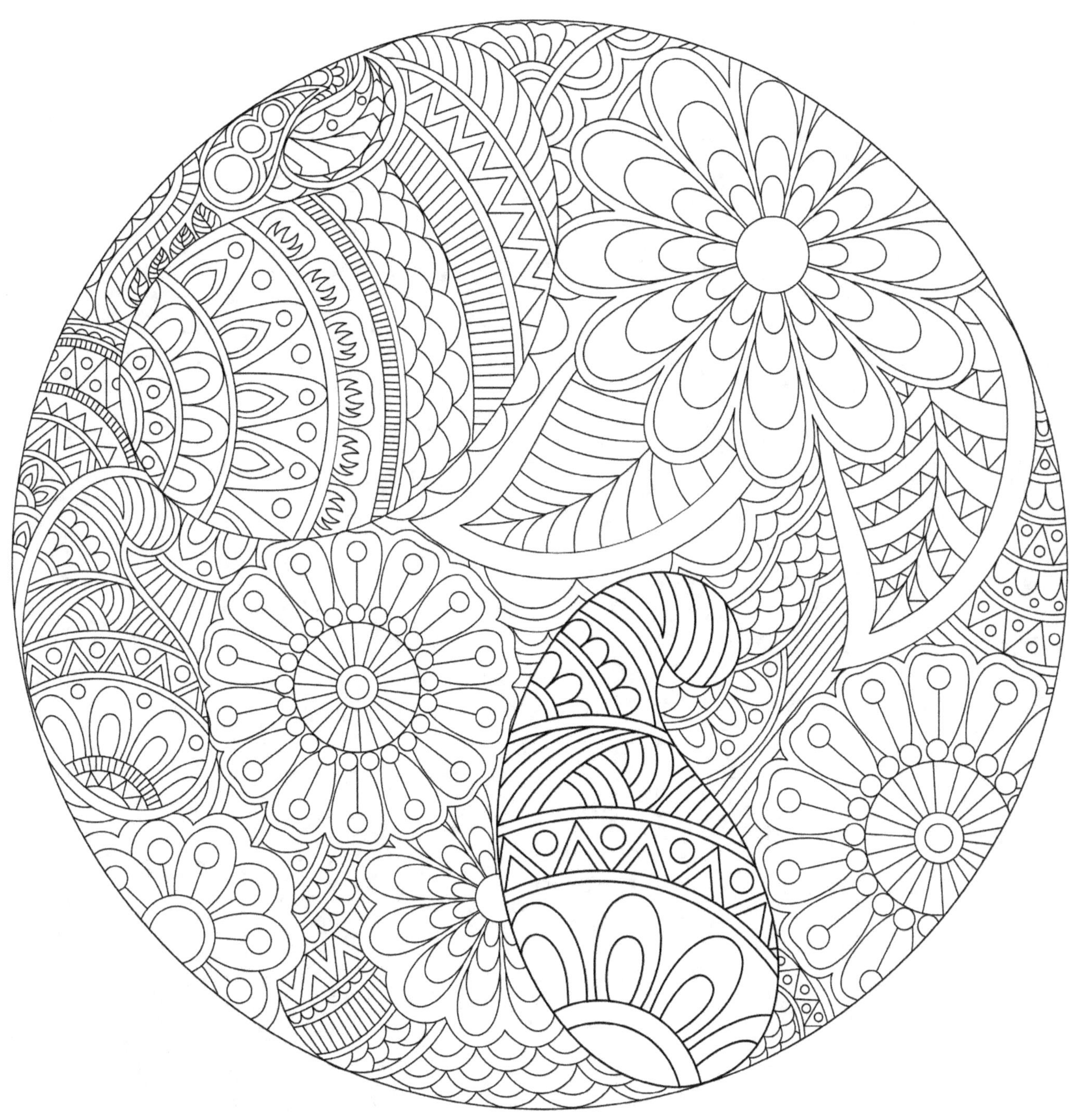

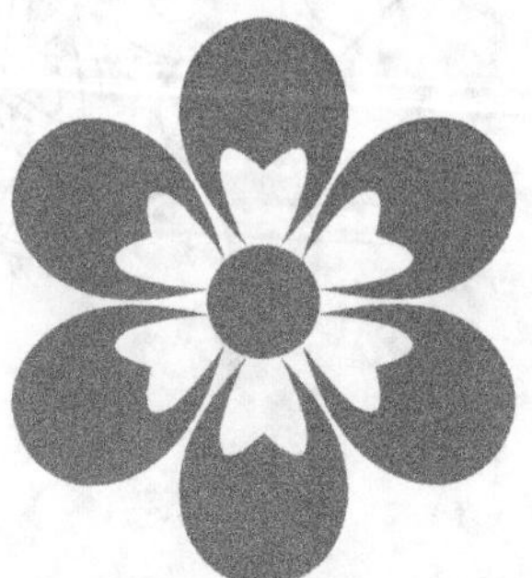

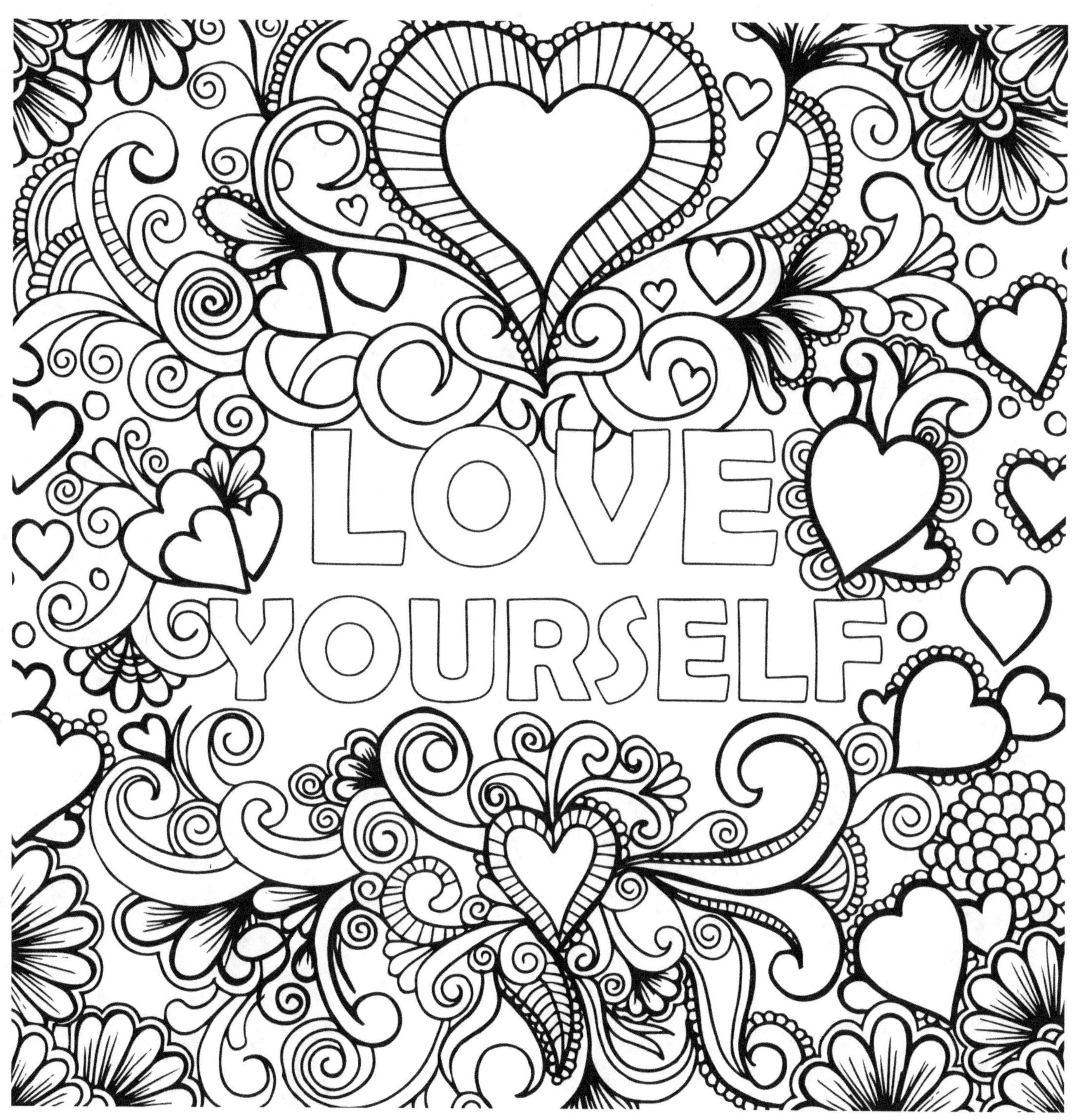

LOVE
YOURSELF

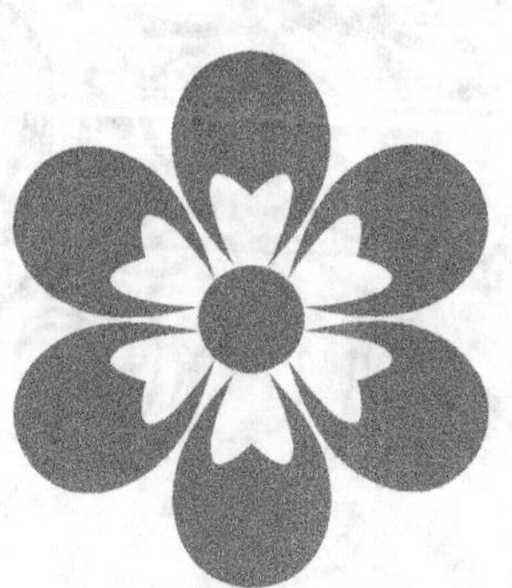

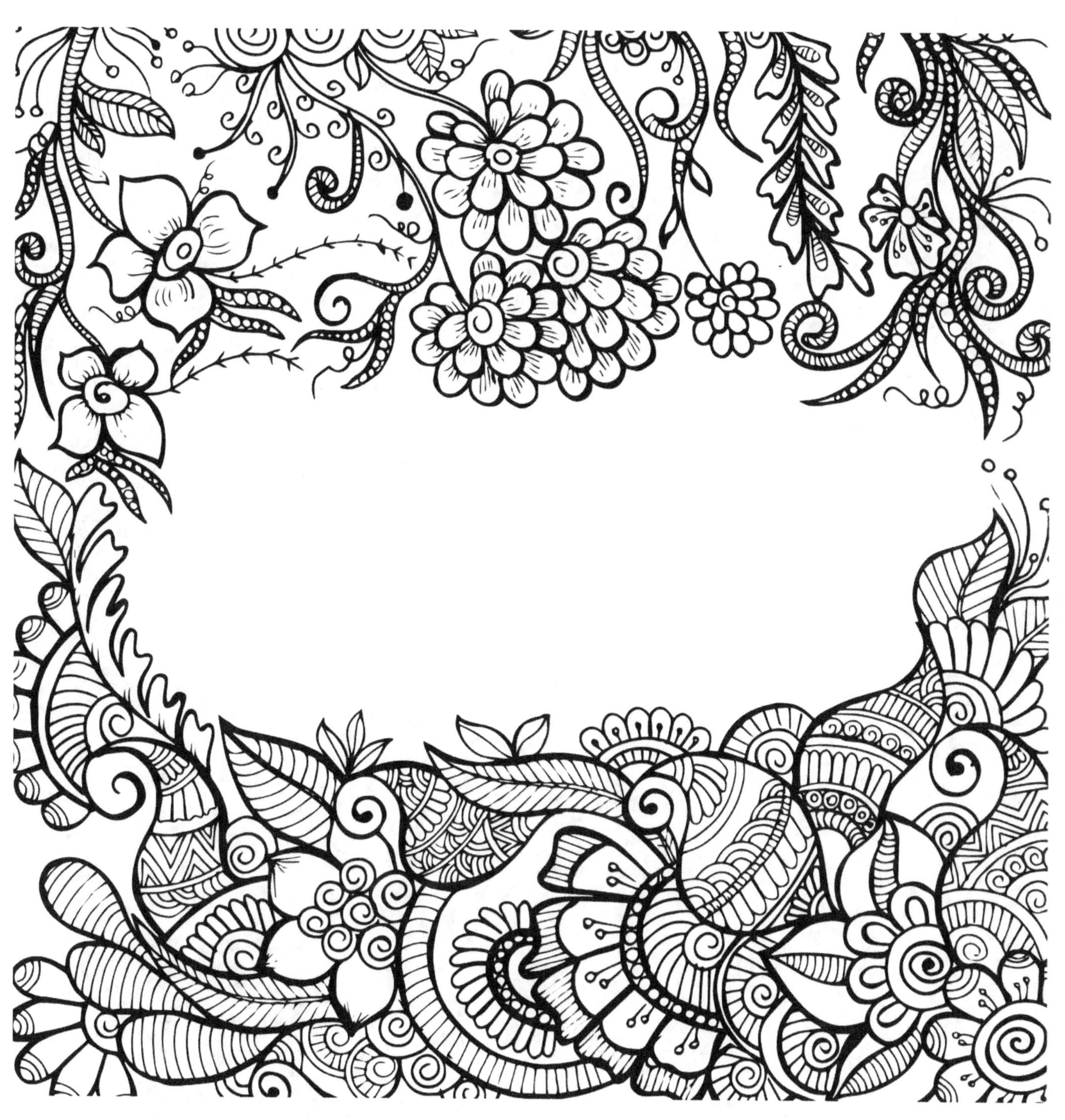

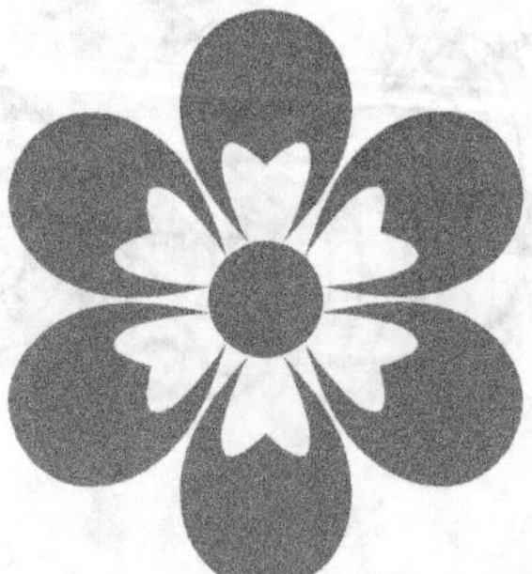

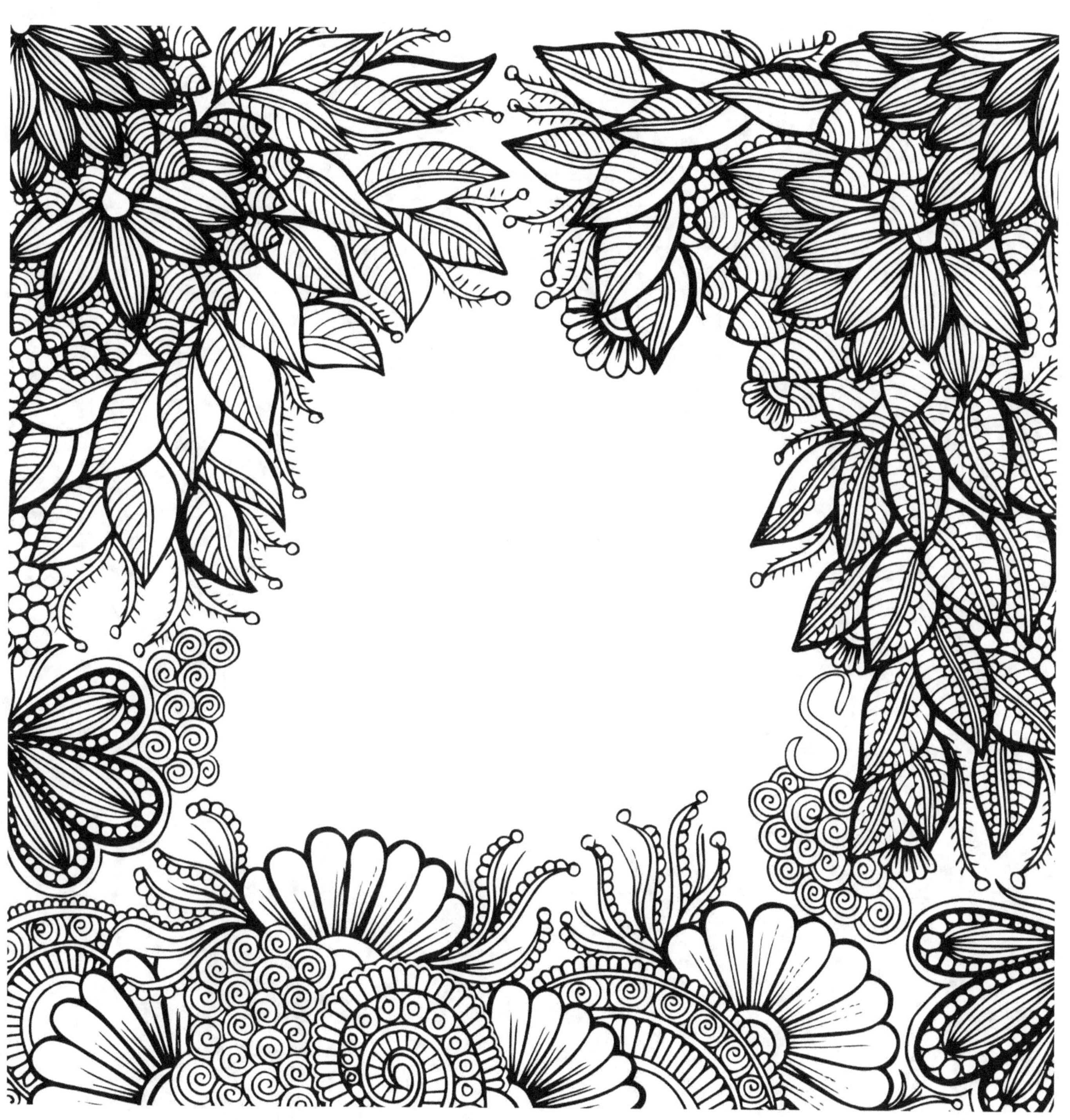

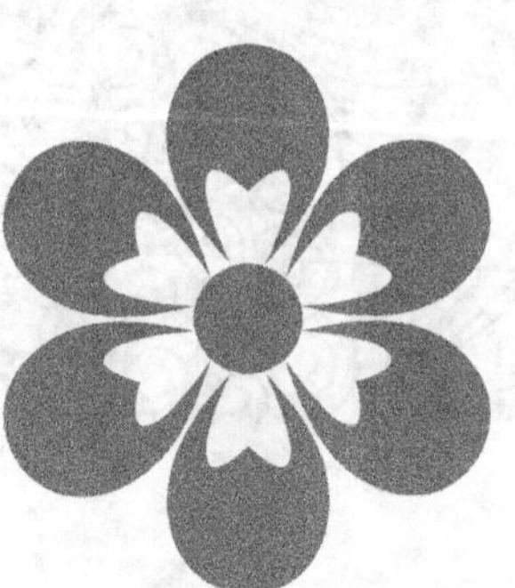

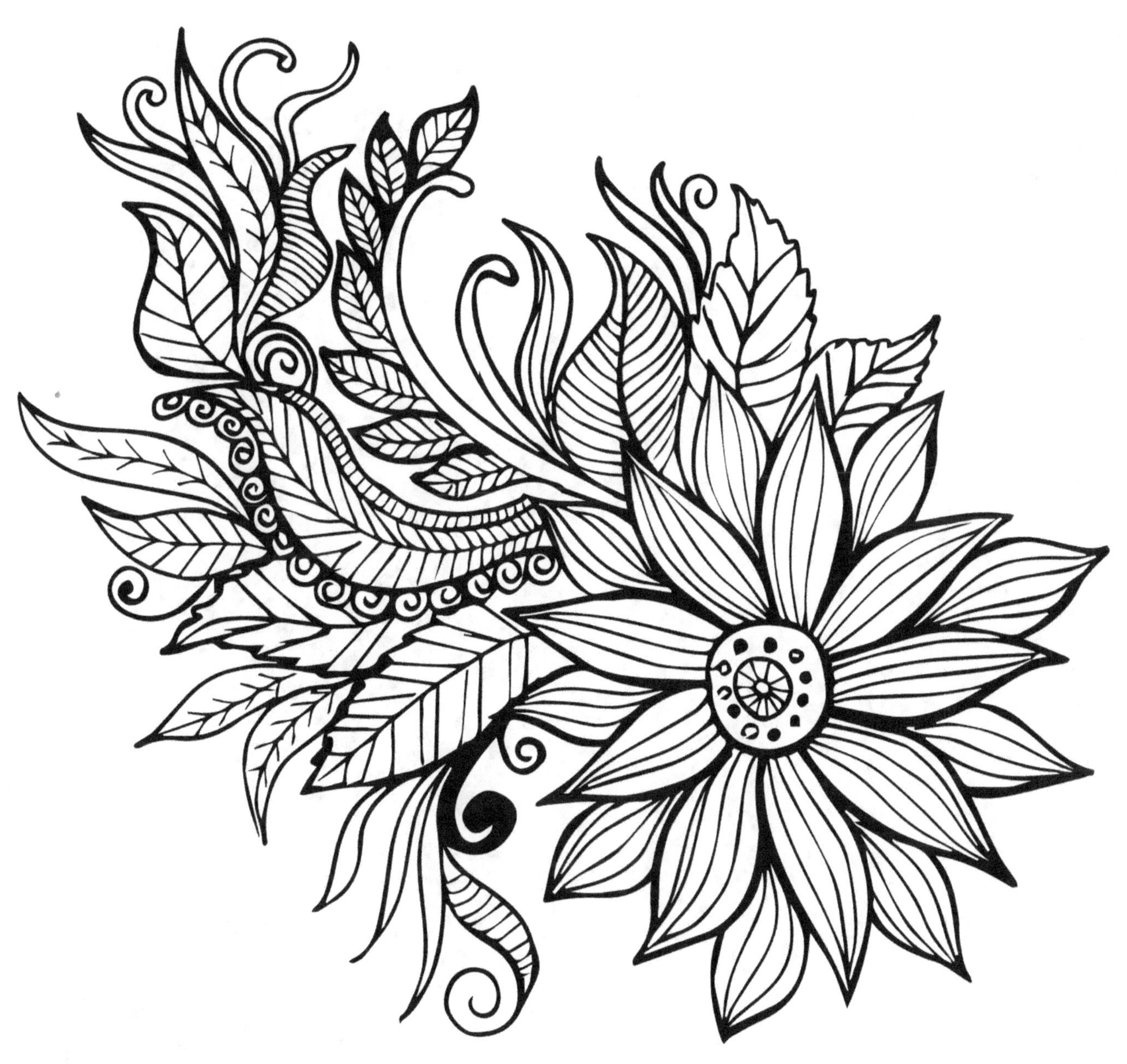

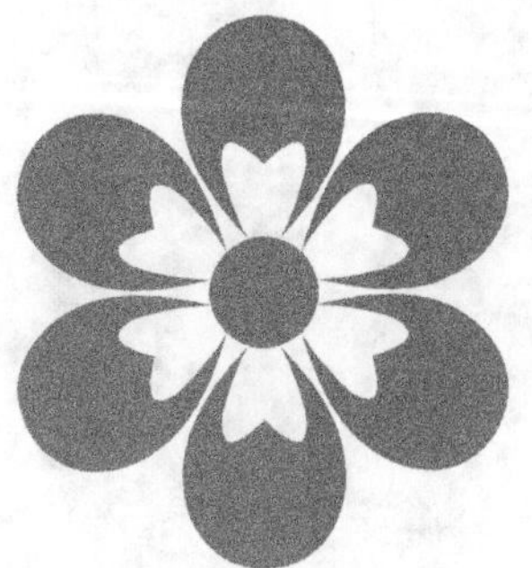

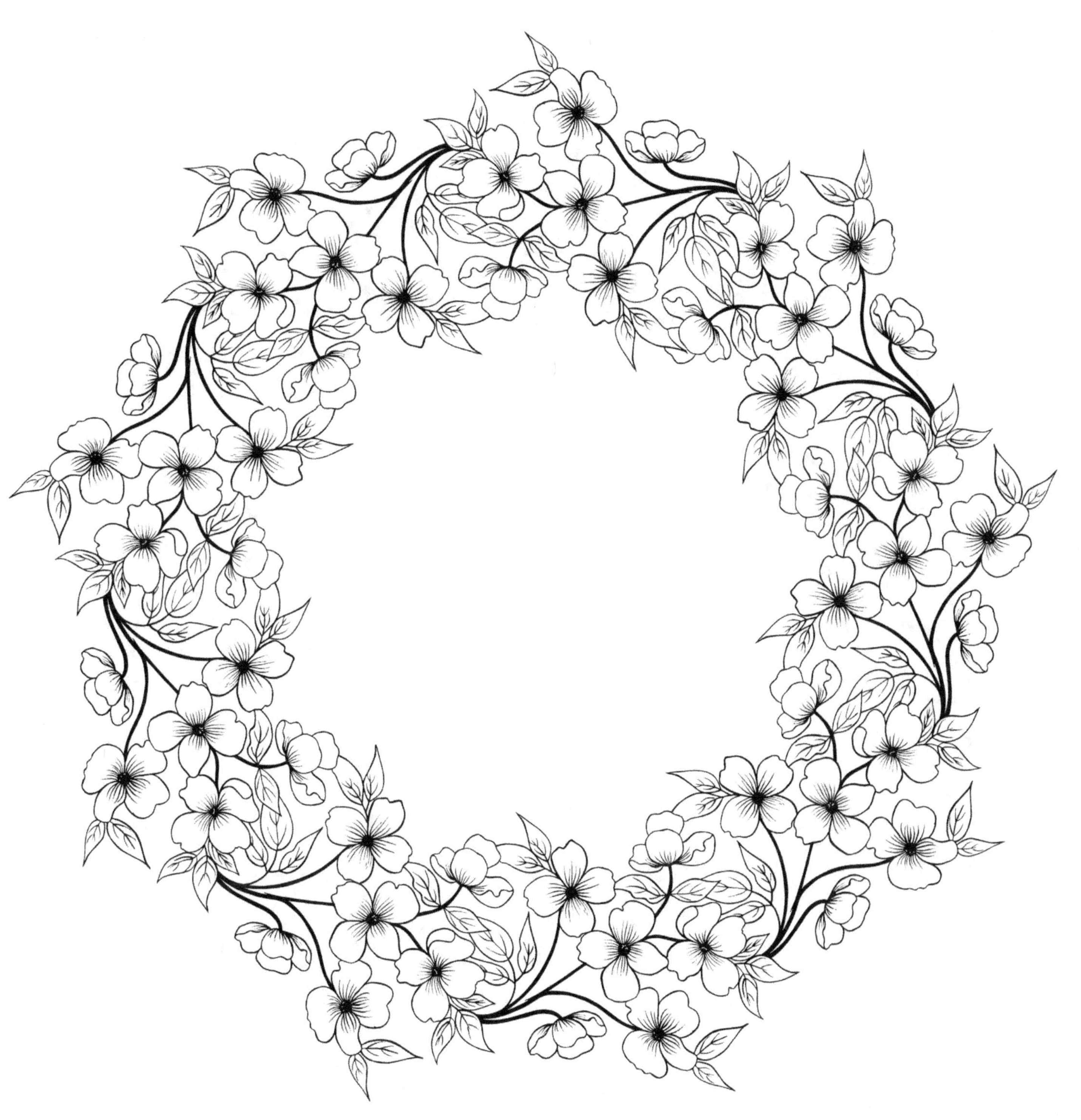

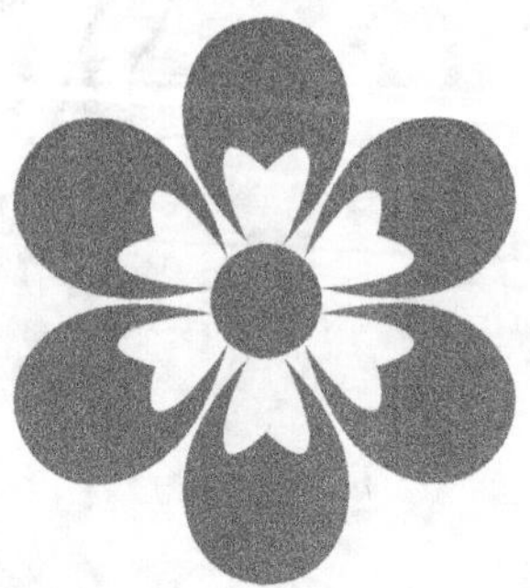

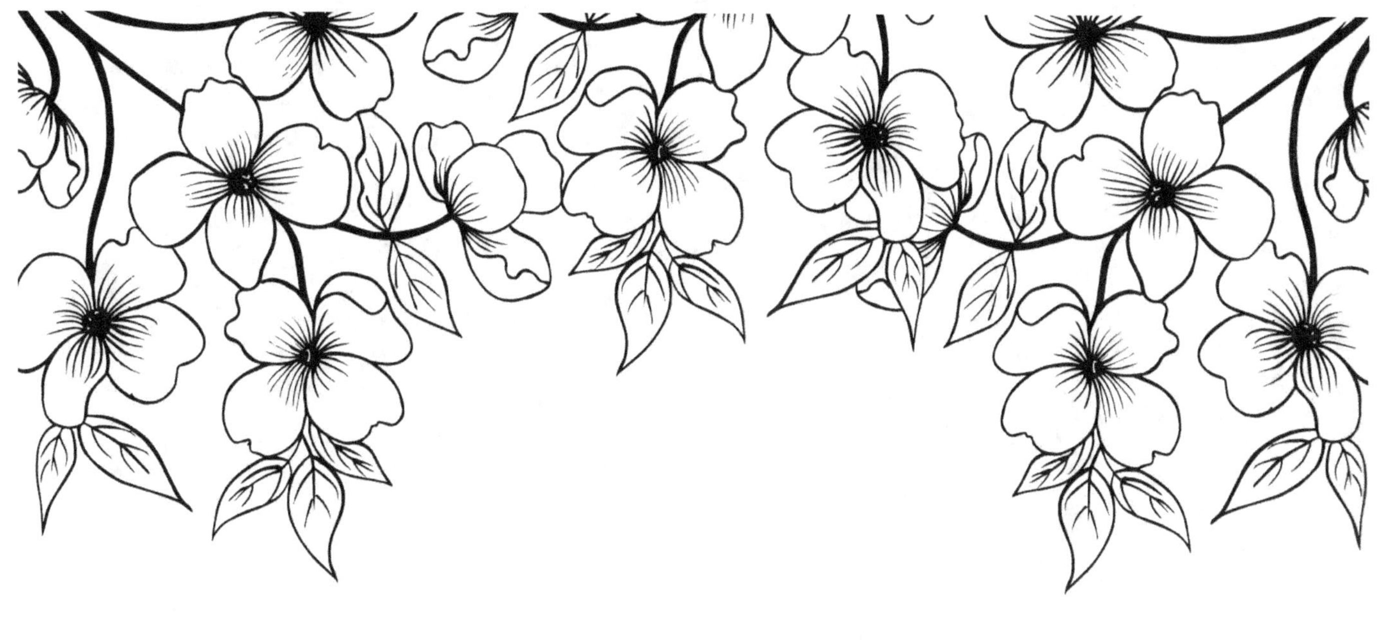

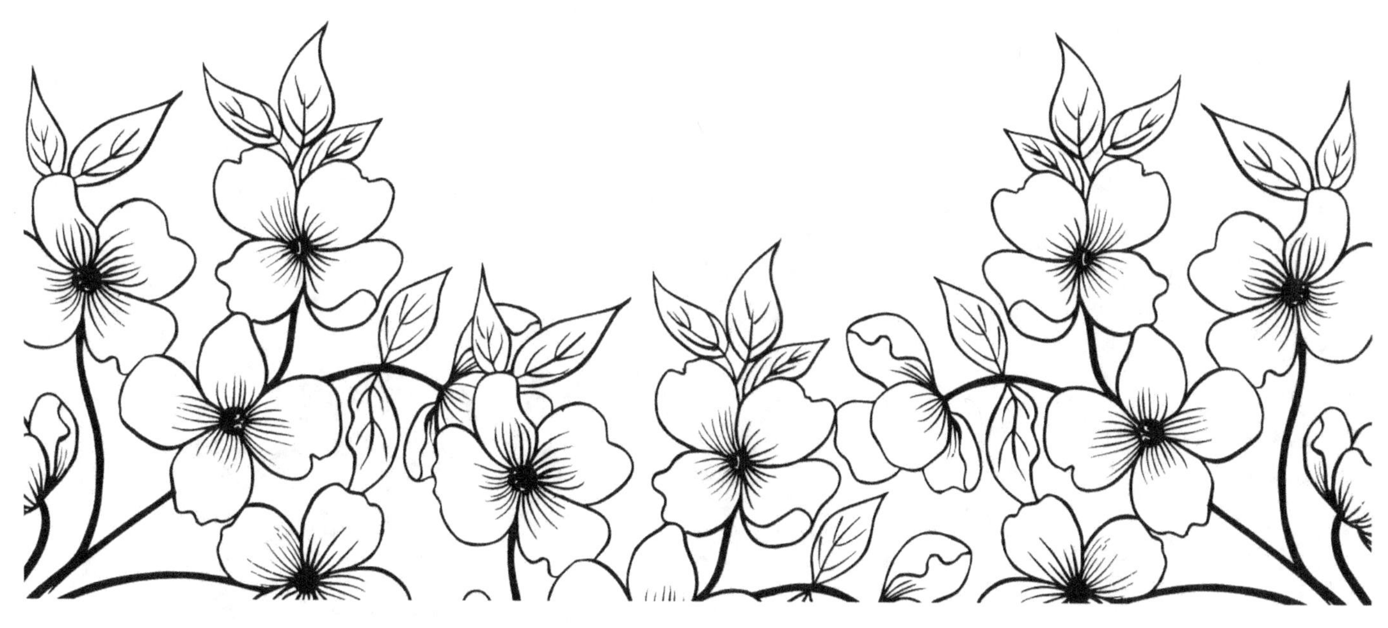

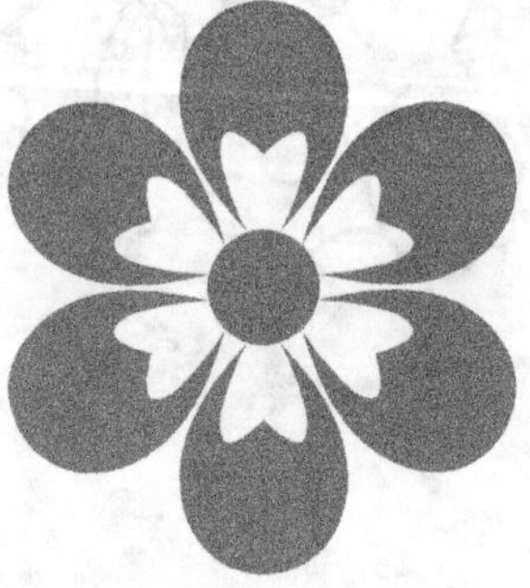

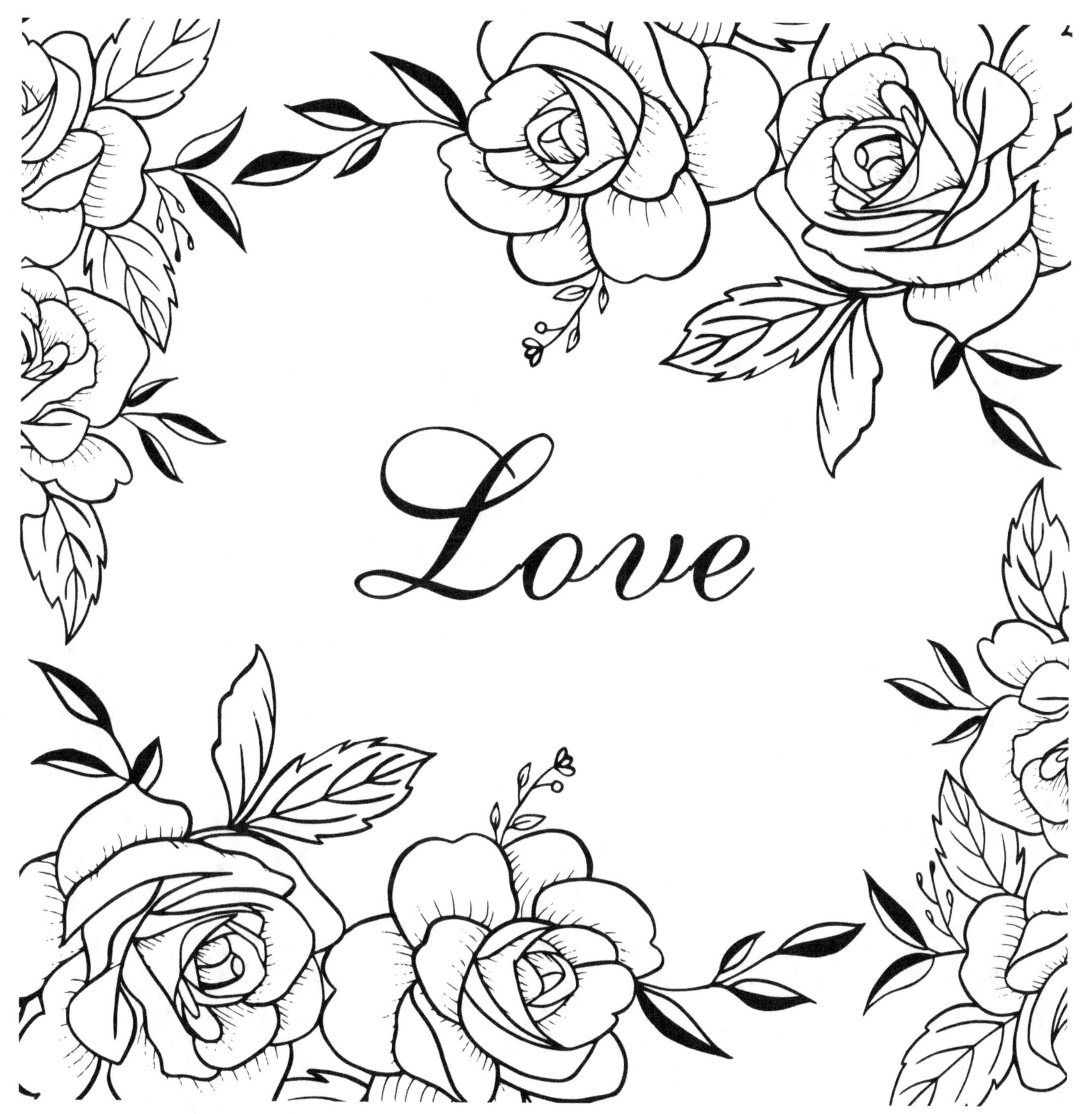

Love

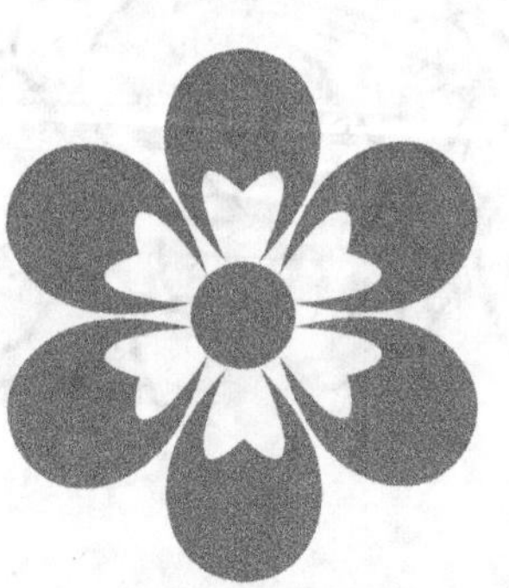

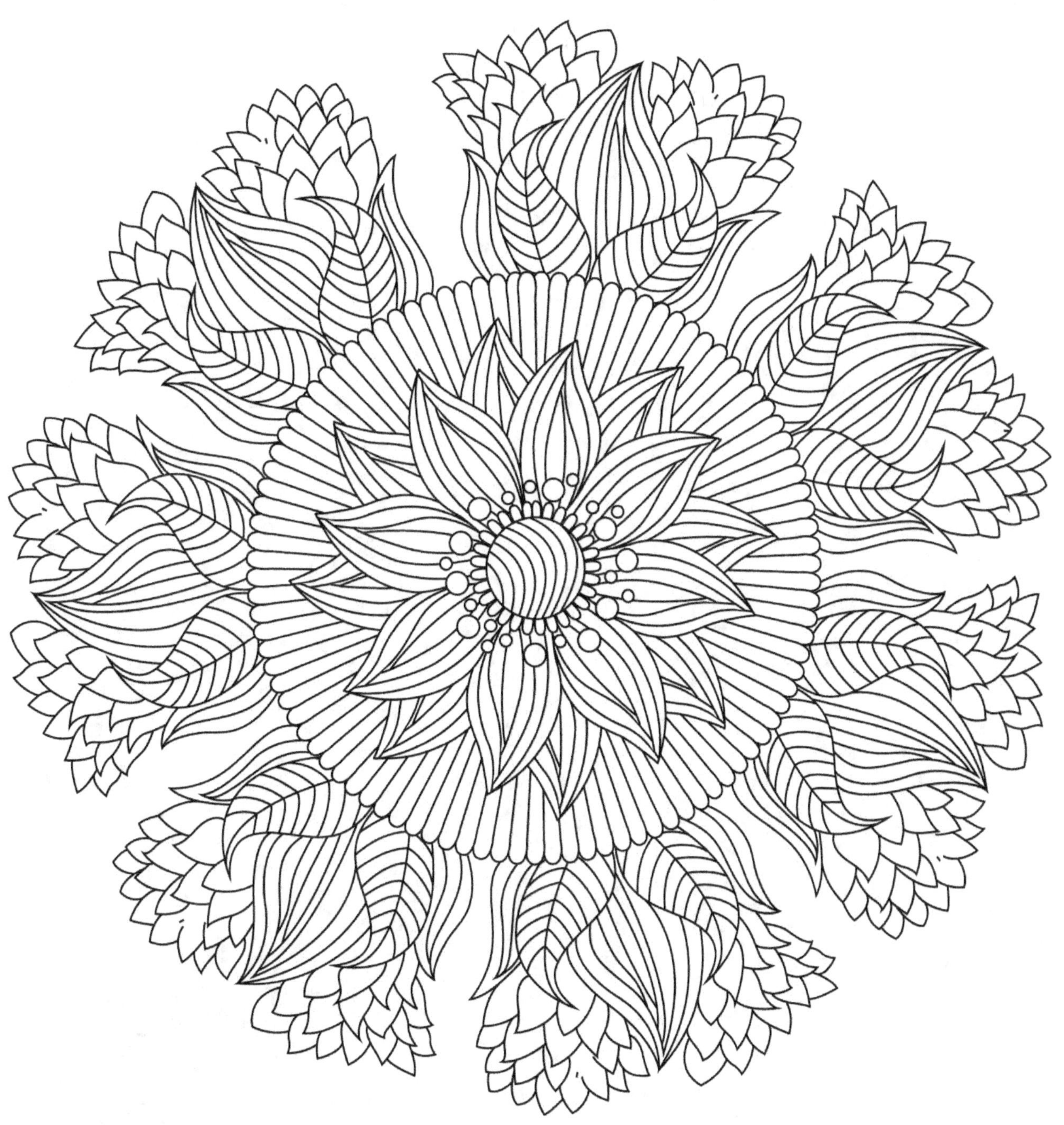

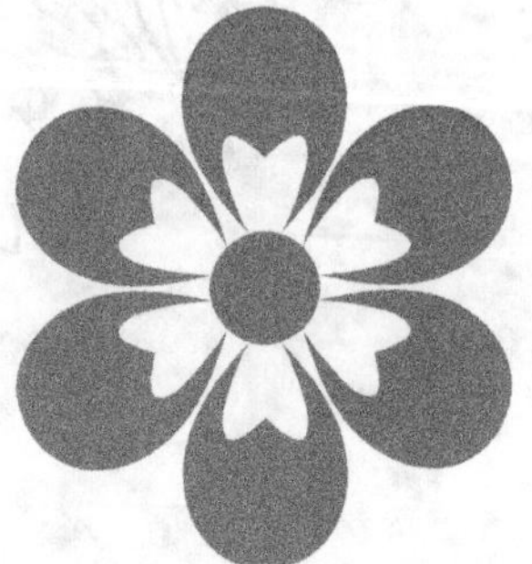

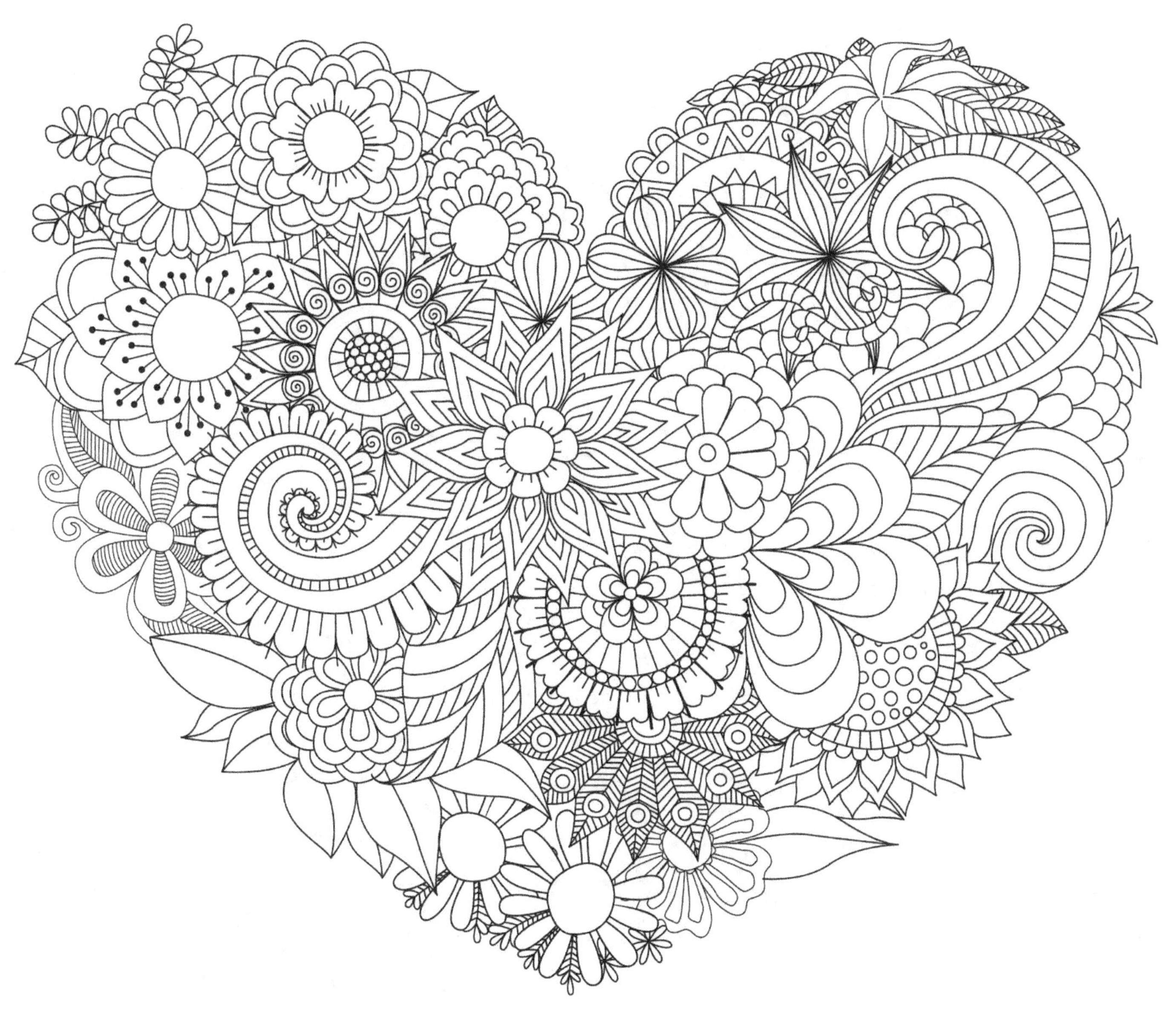

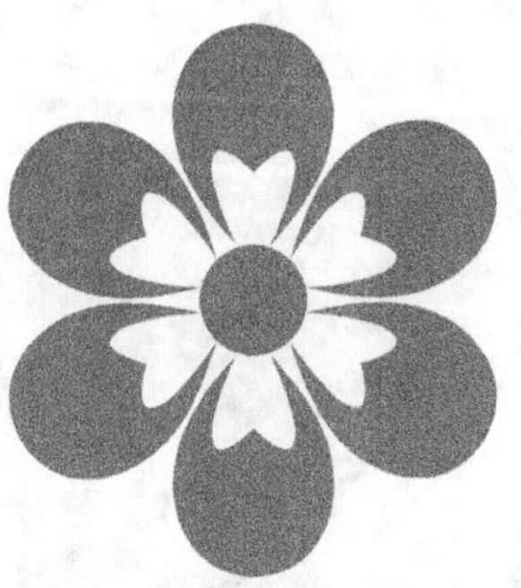

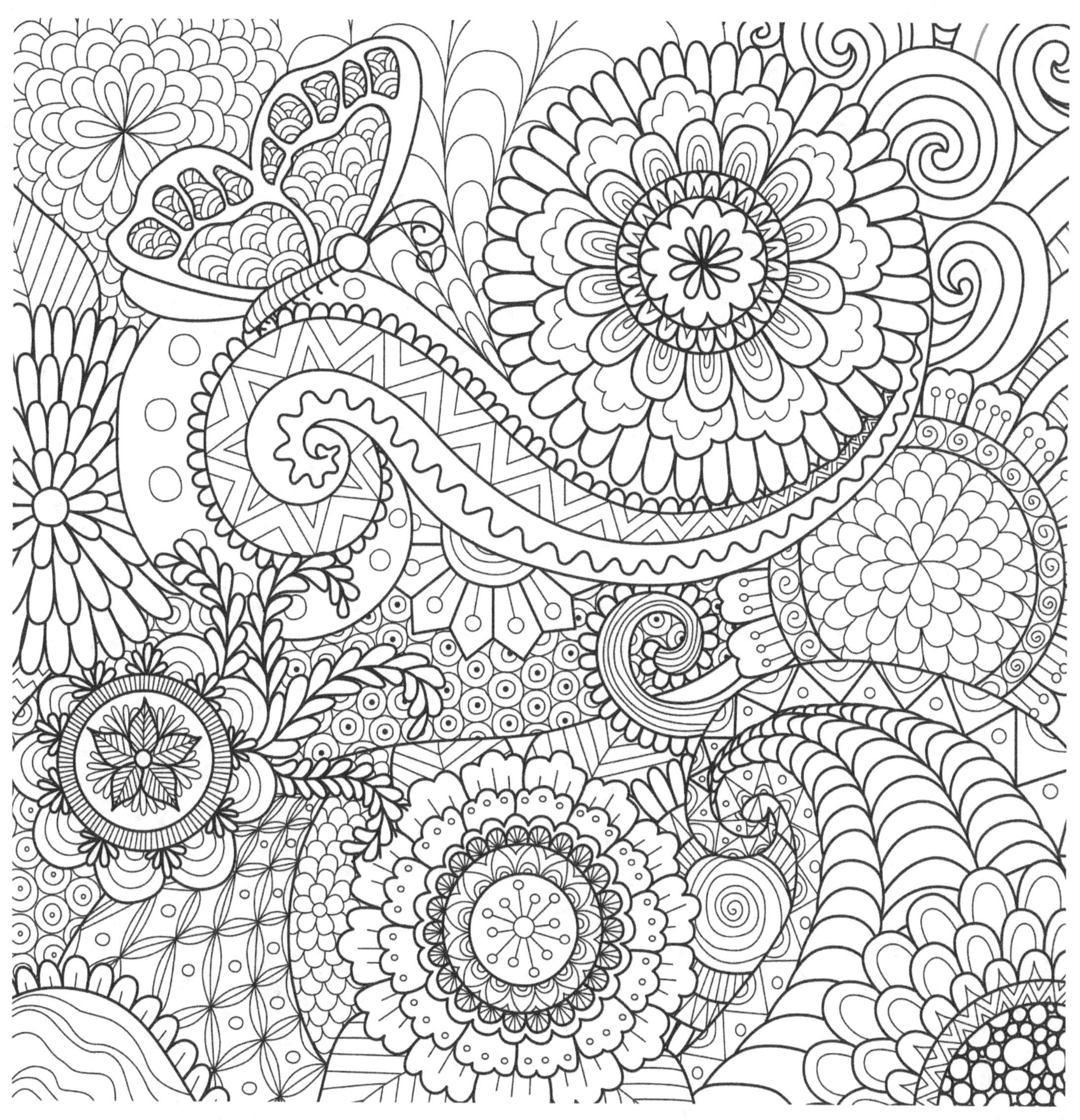

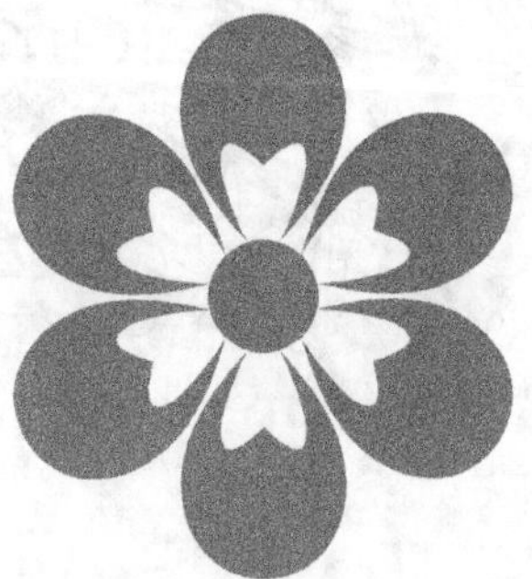

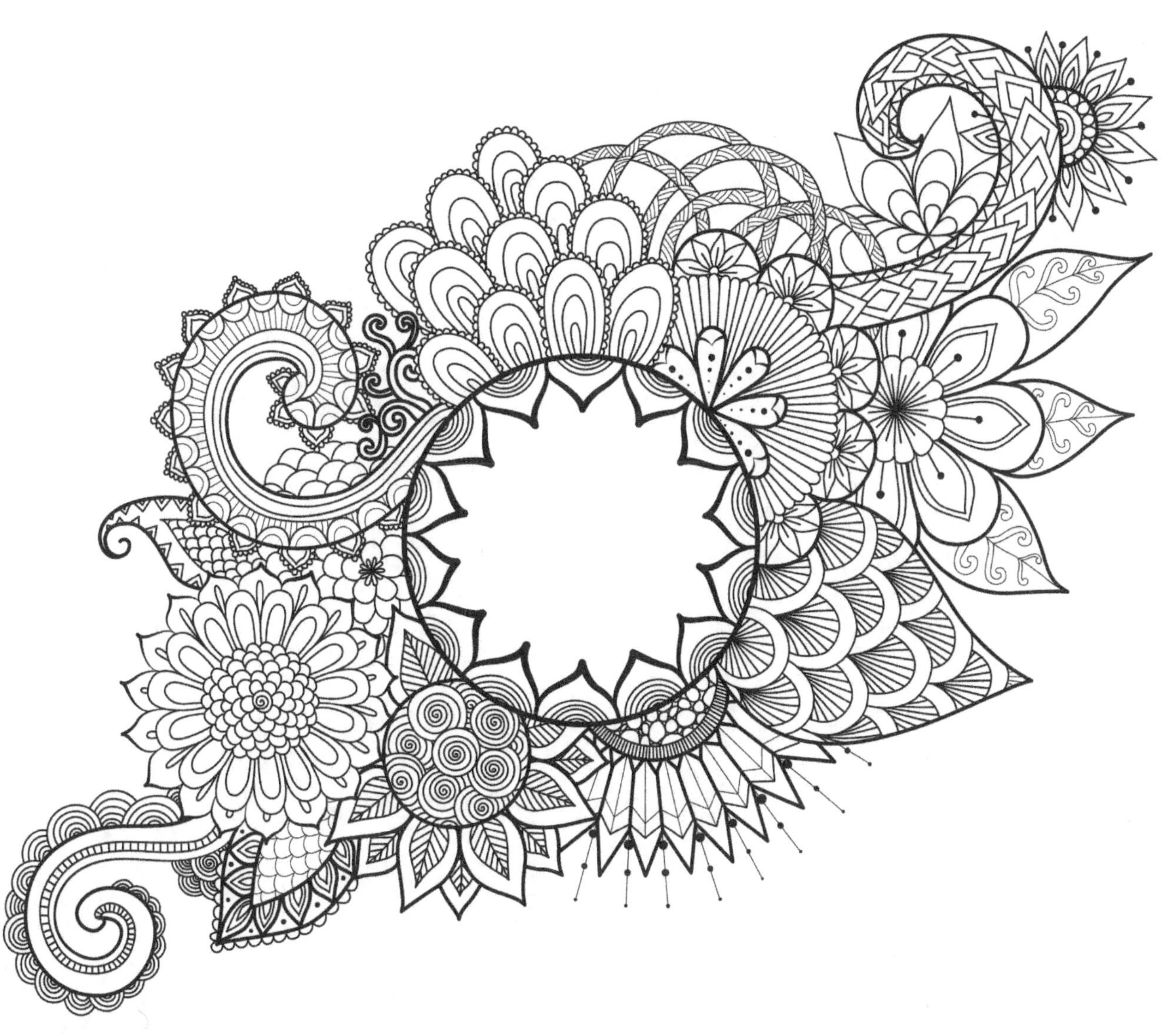

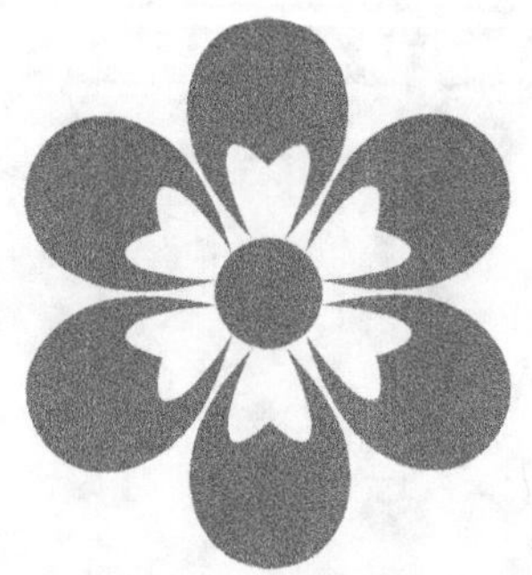

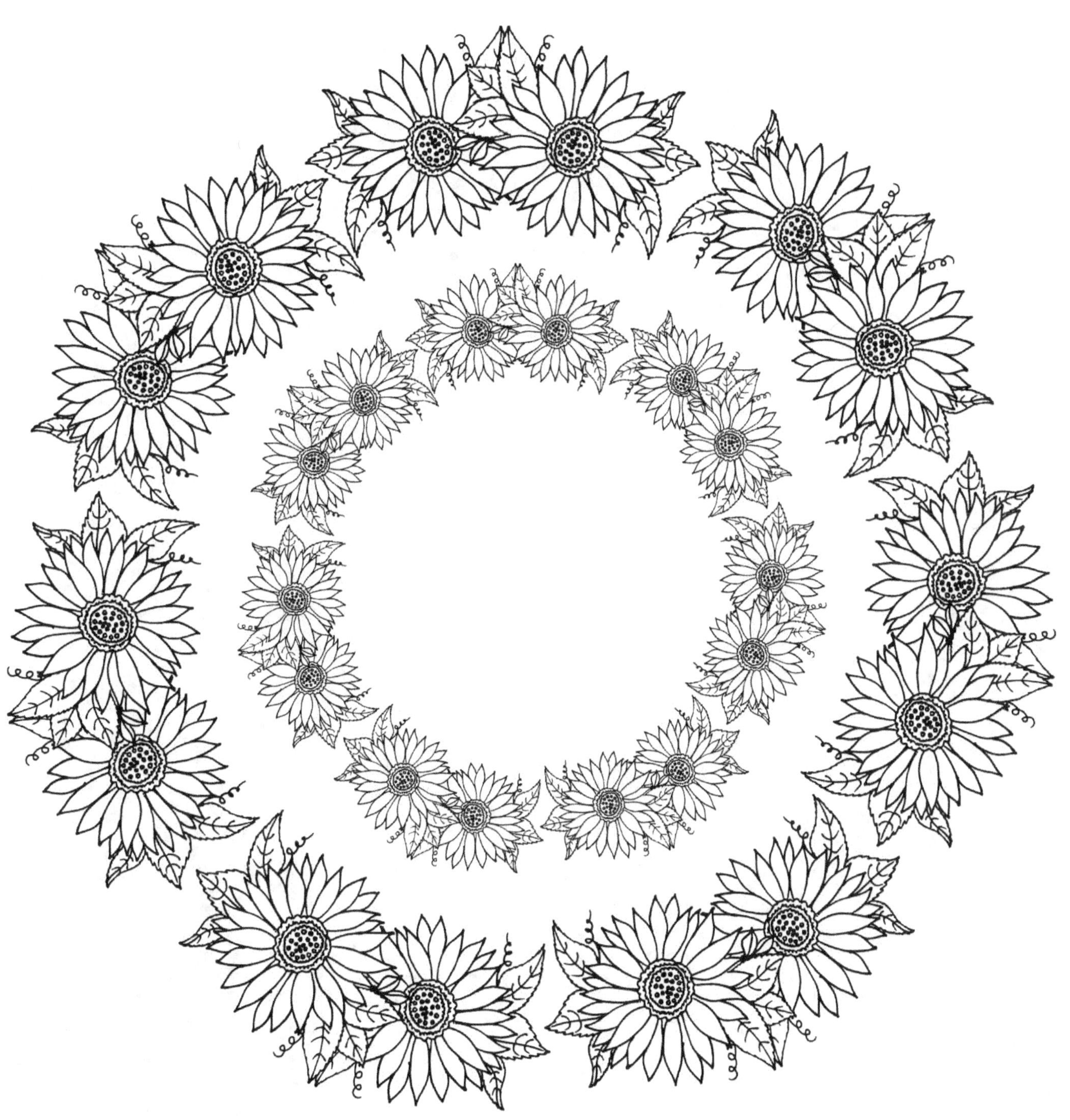

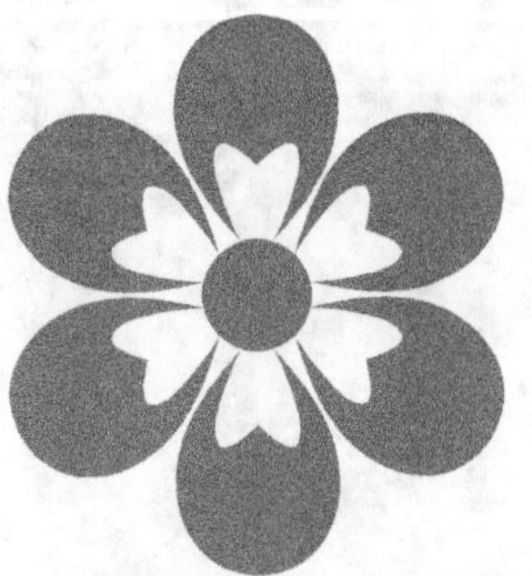

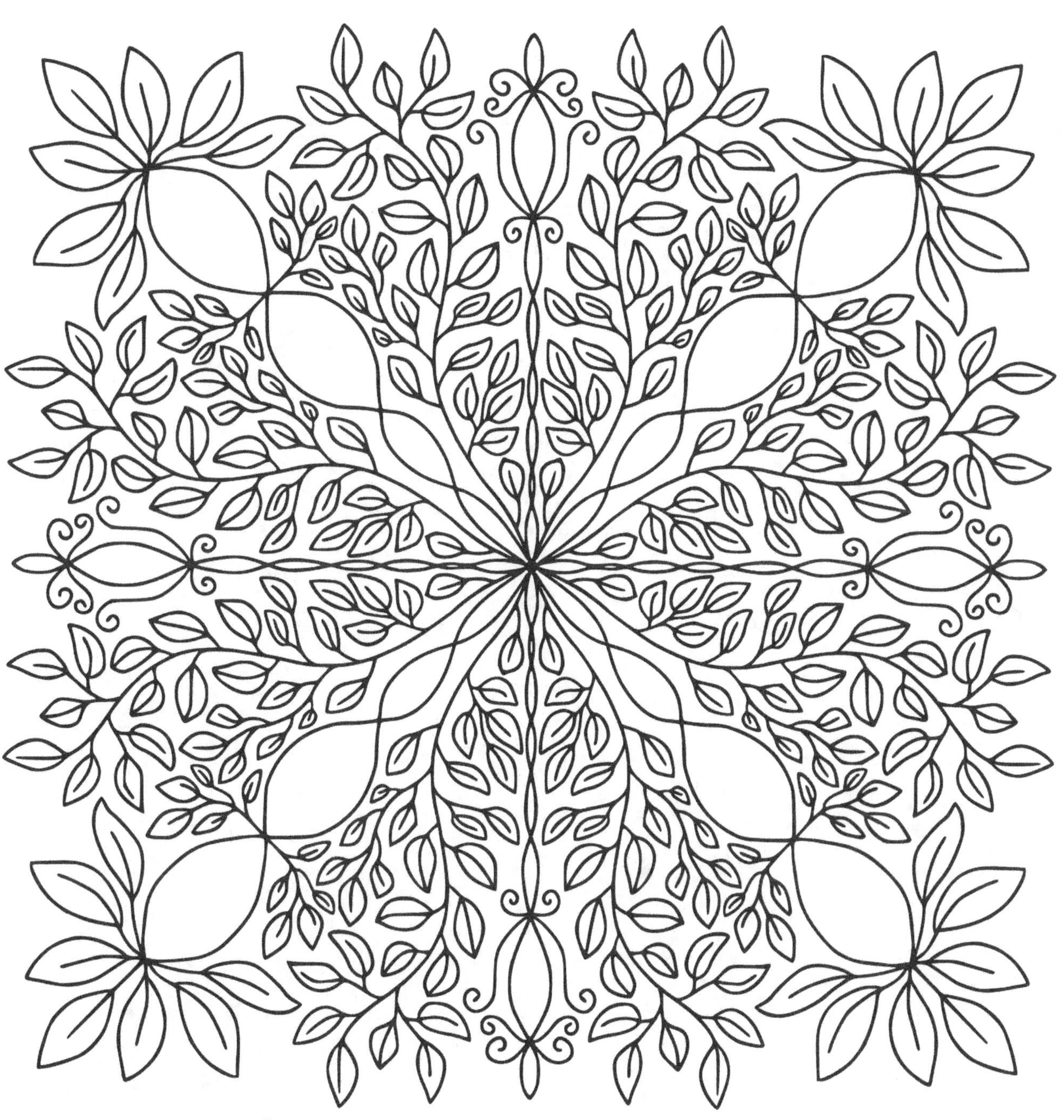

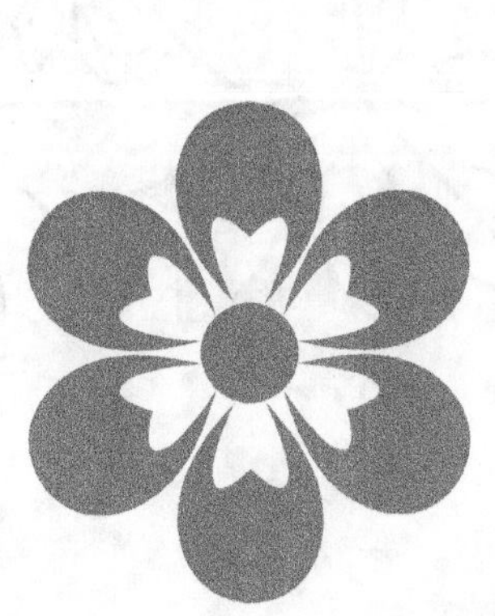

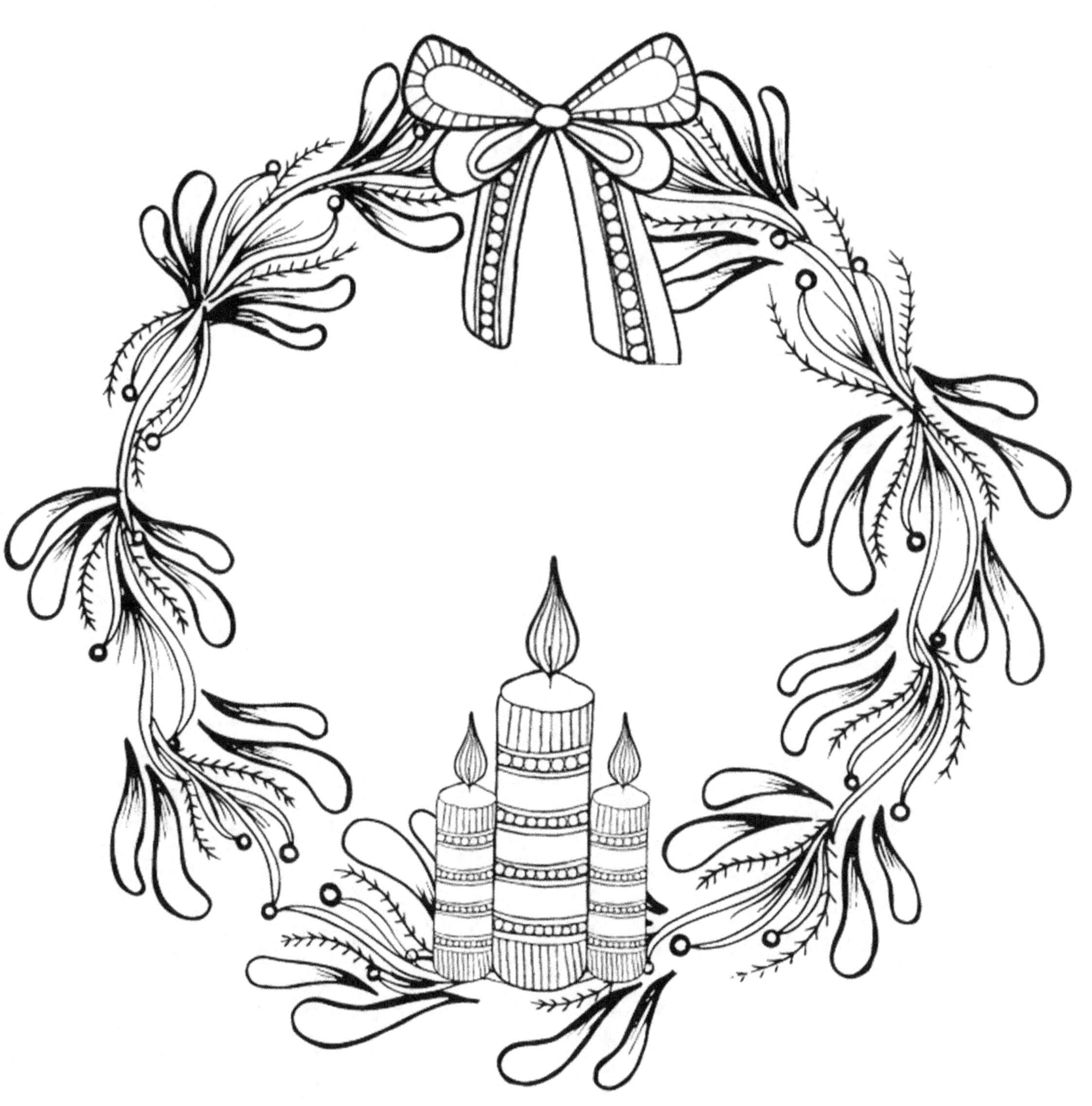

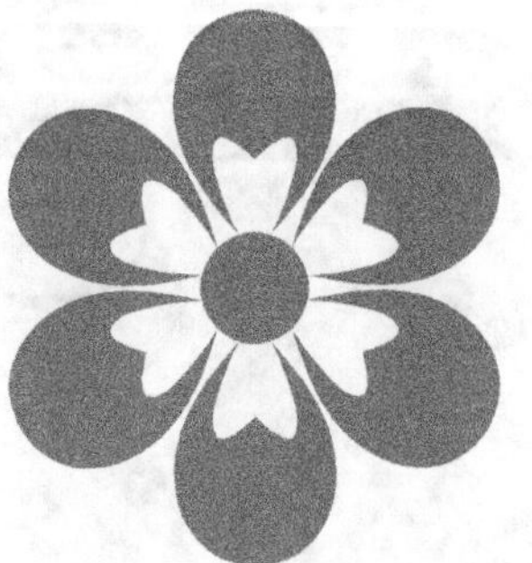

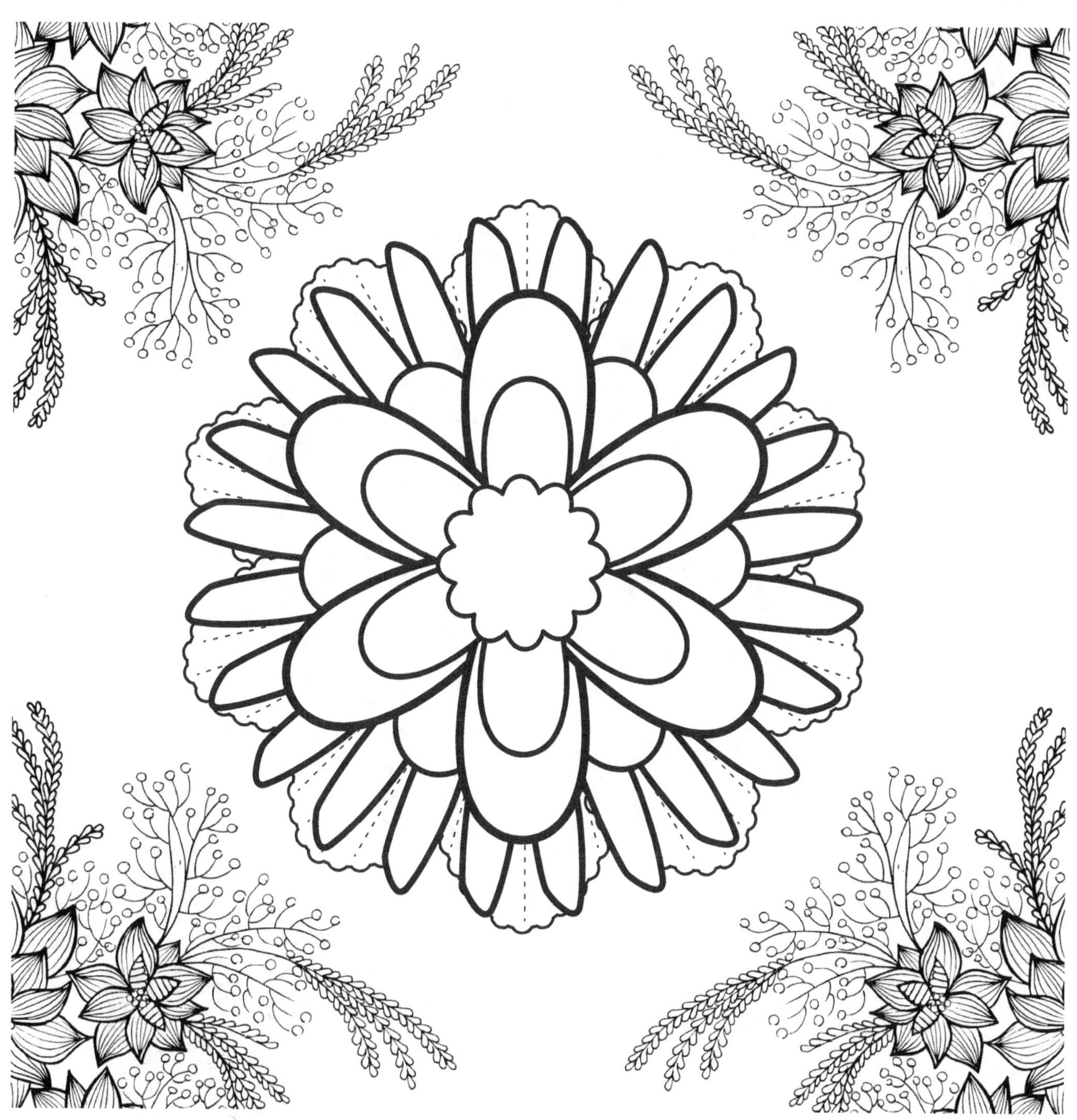

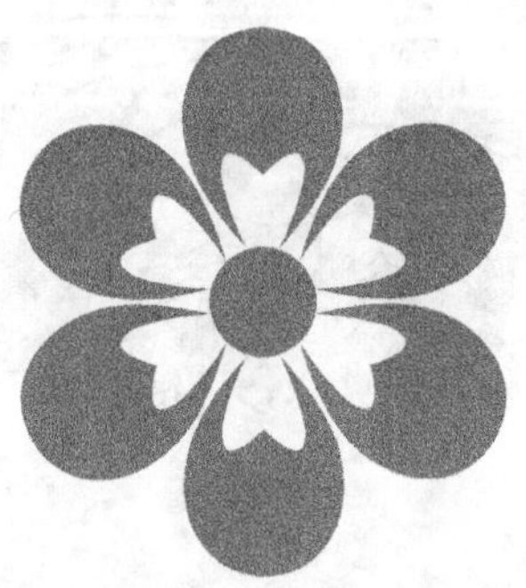

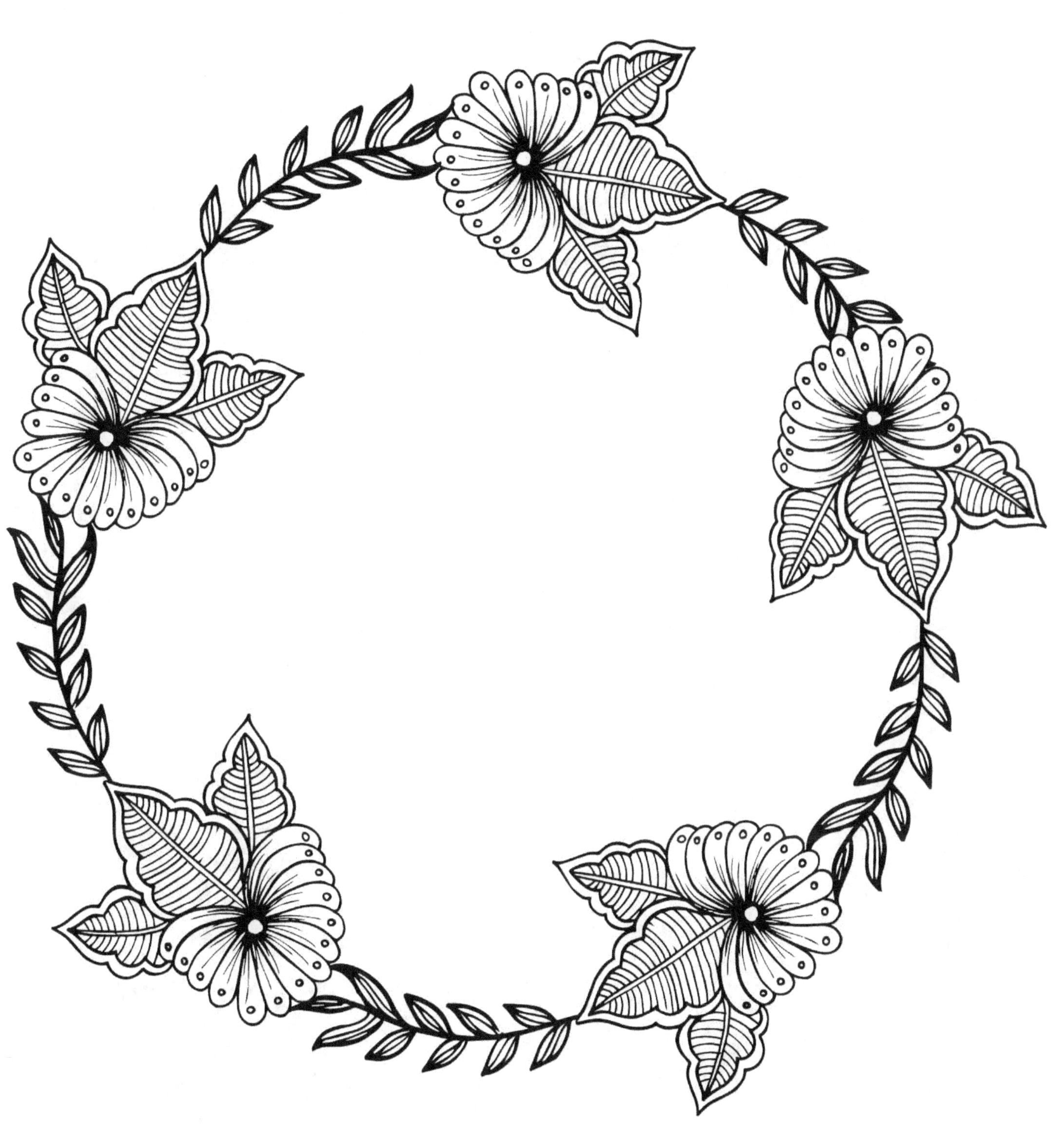

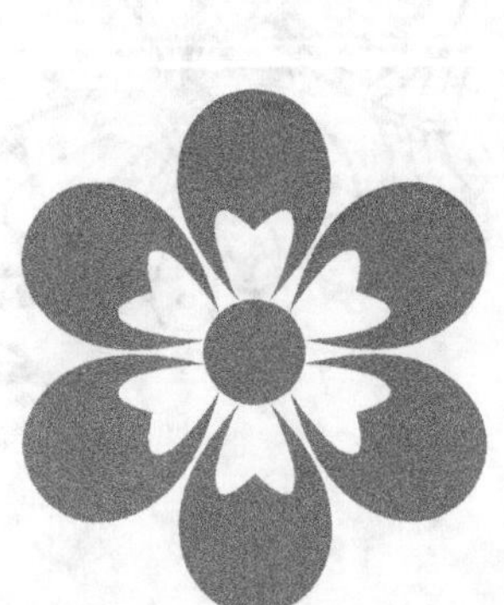

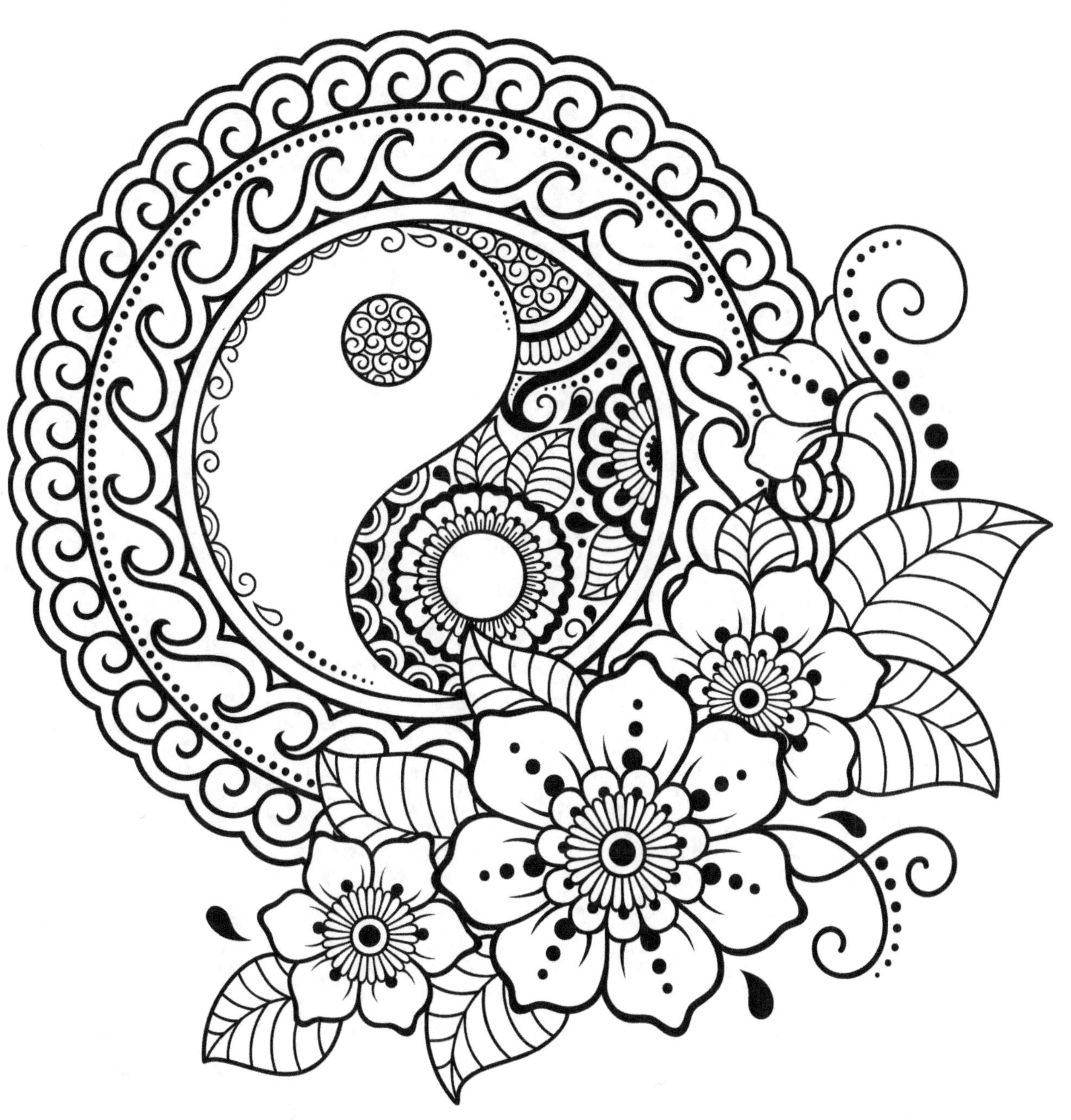

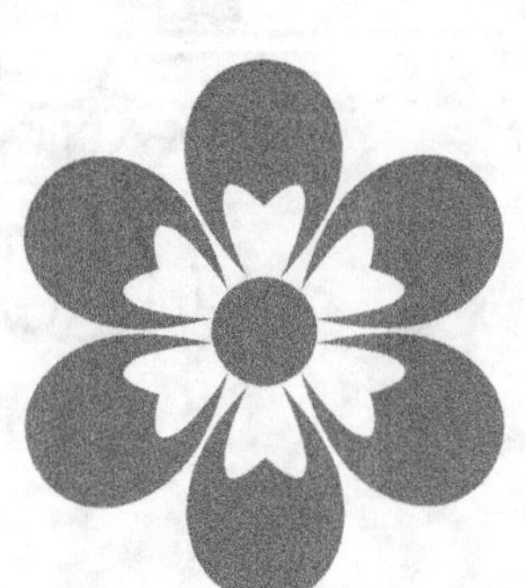

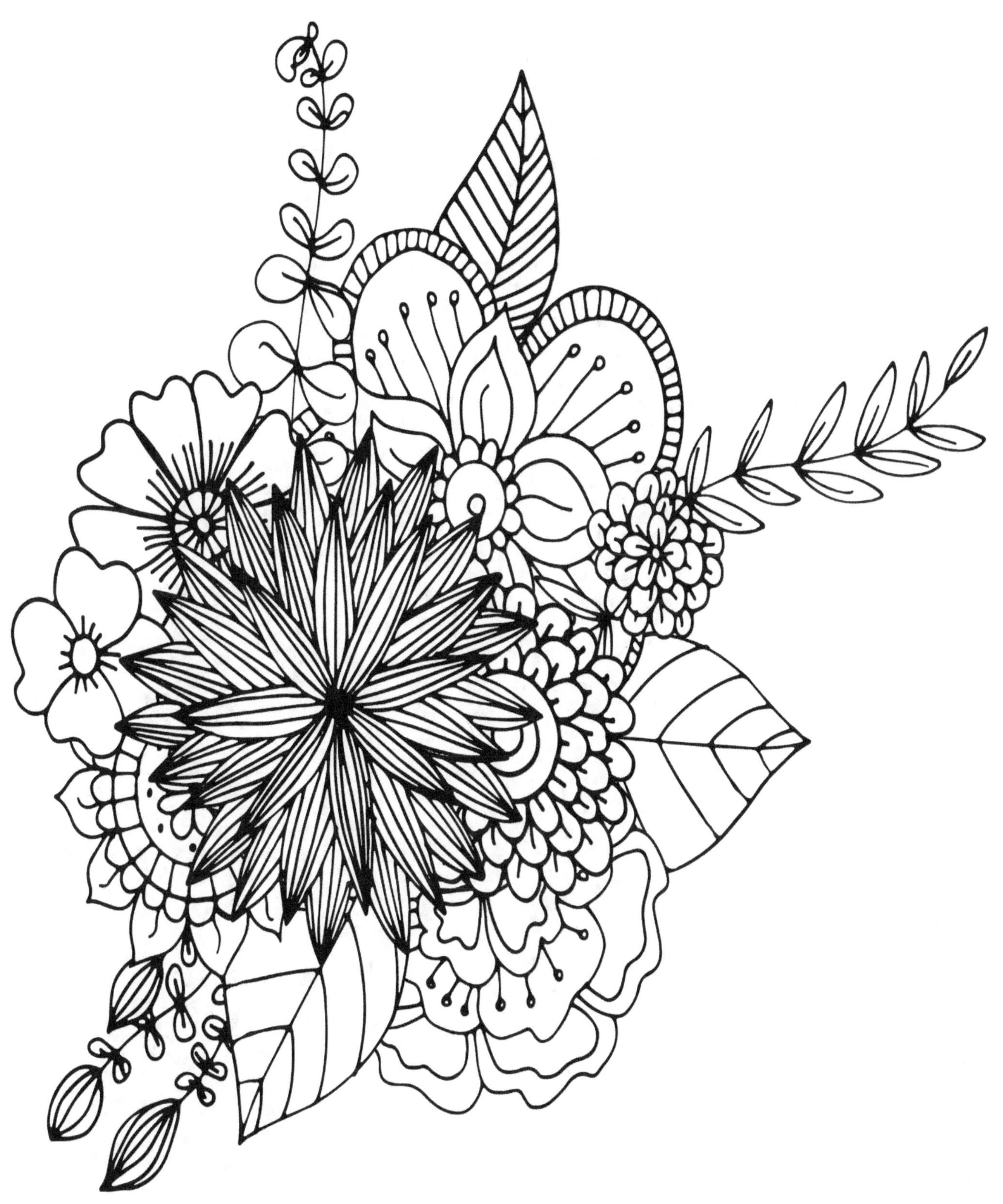

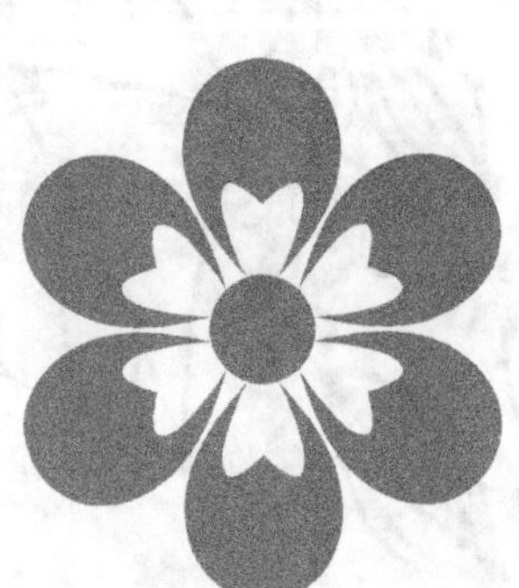

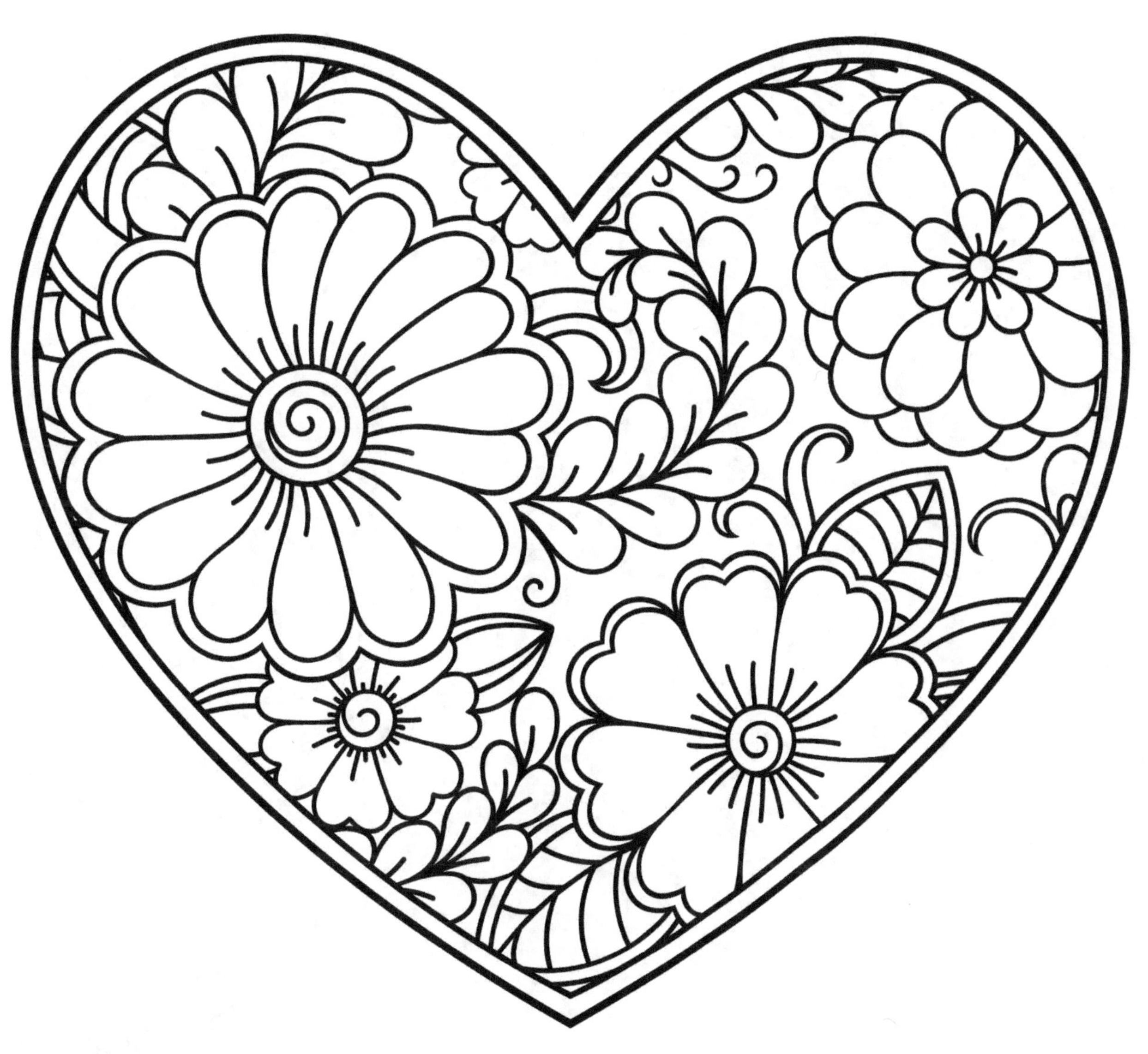

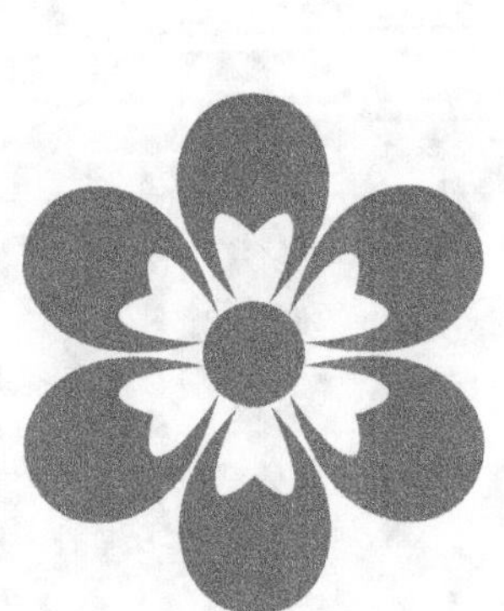

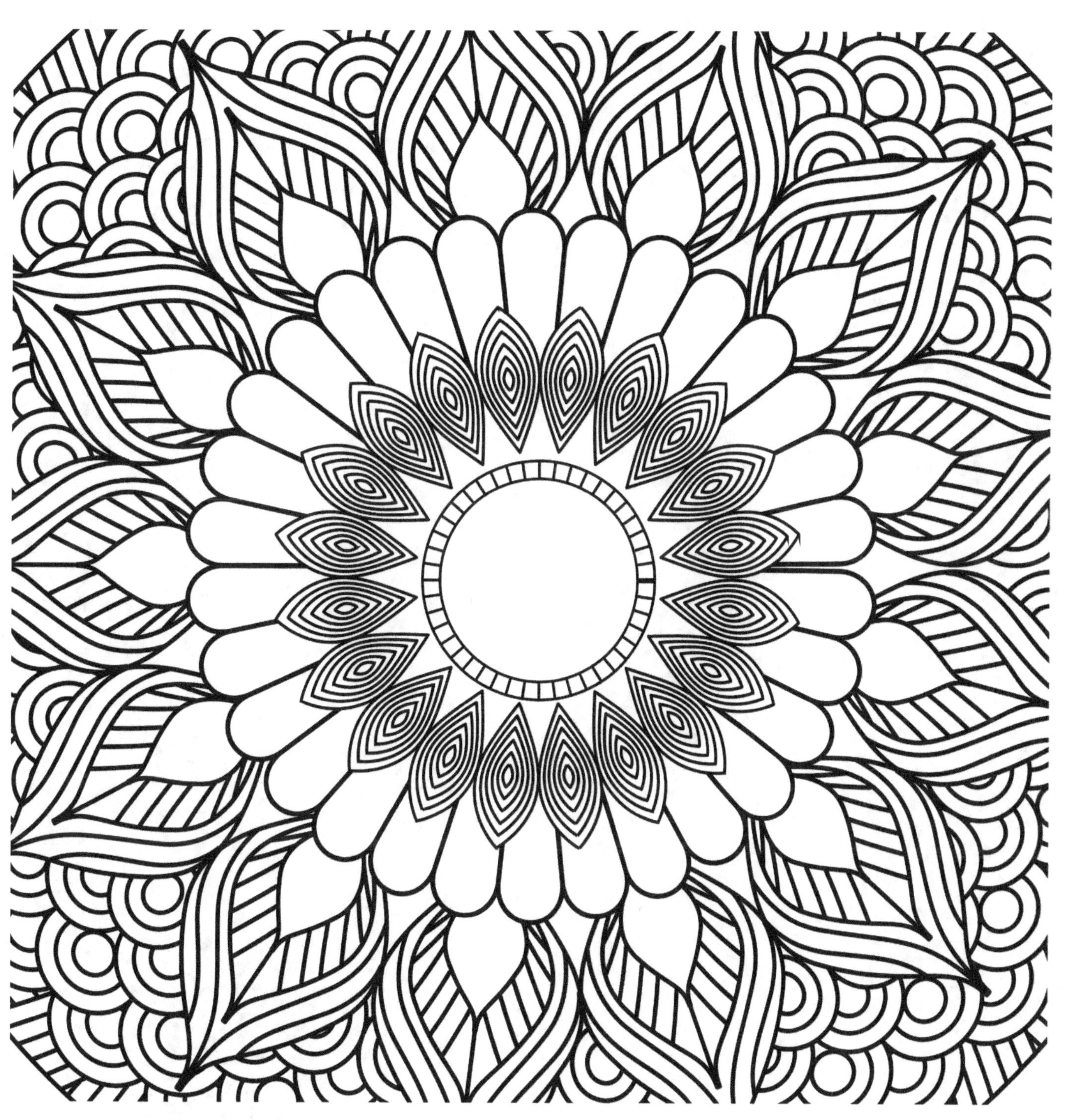

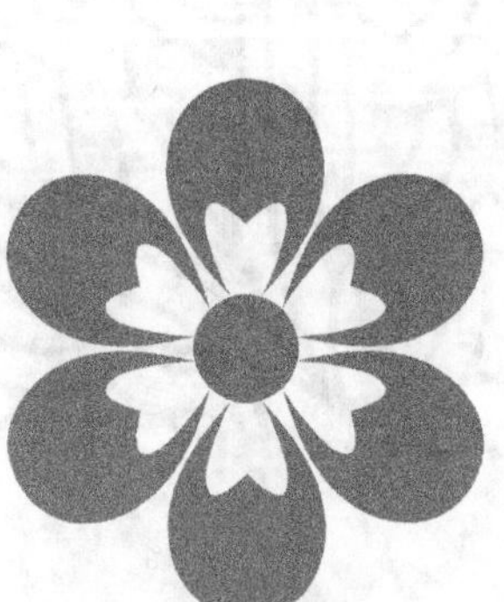

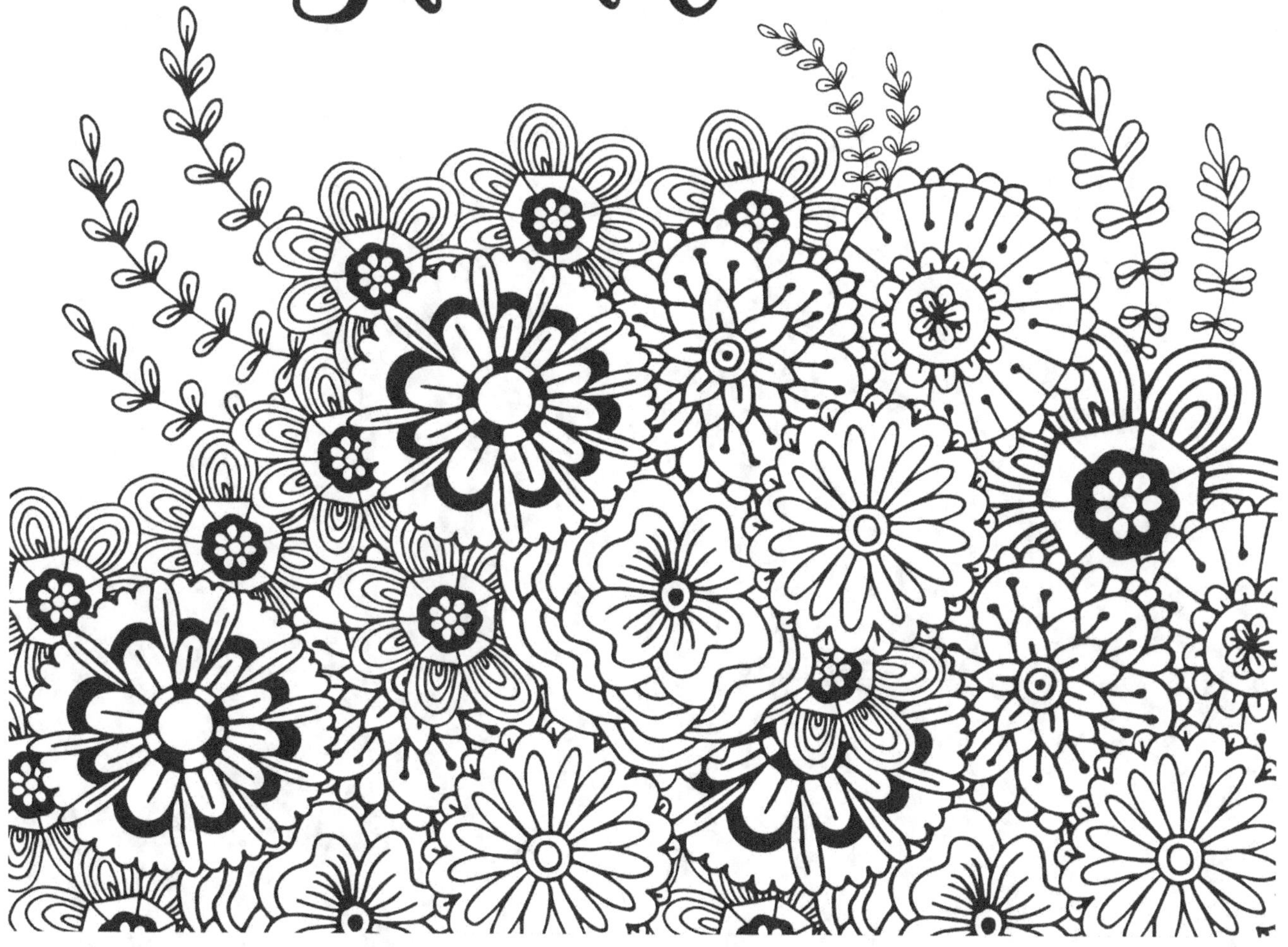

hello
summer

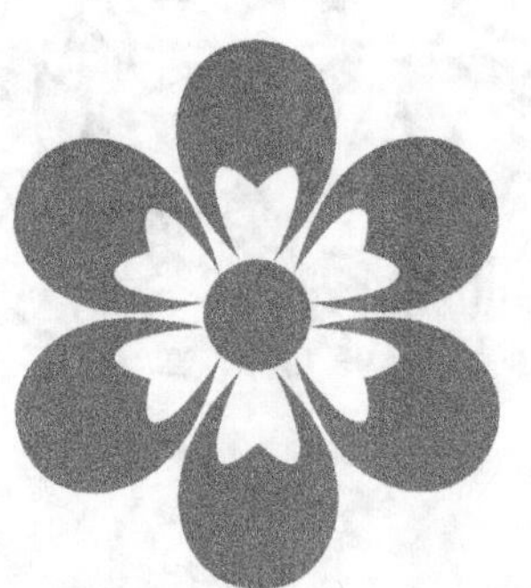

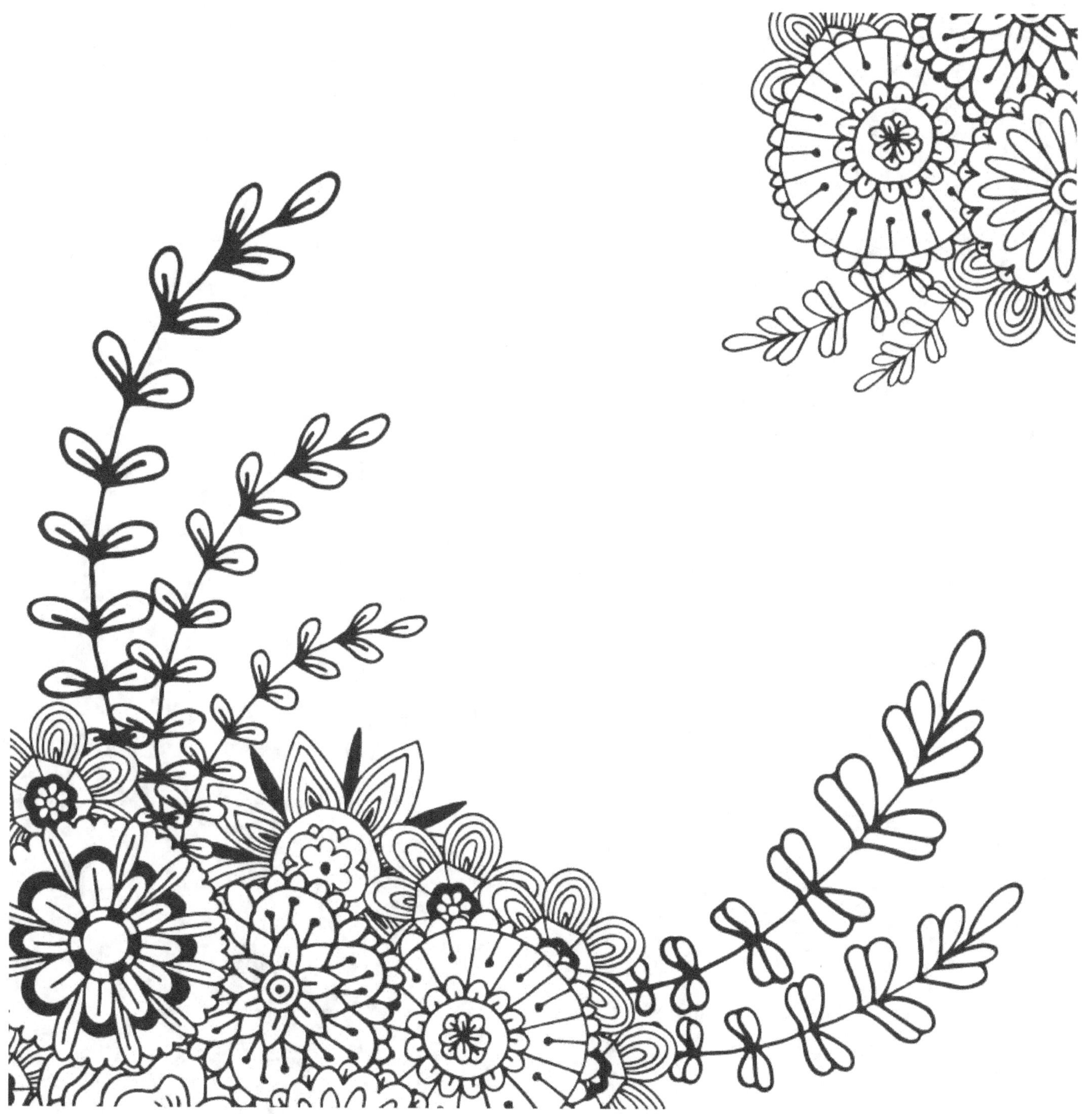

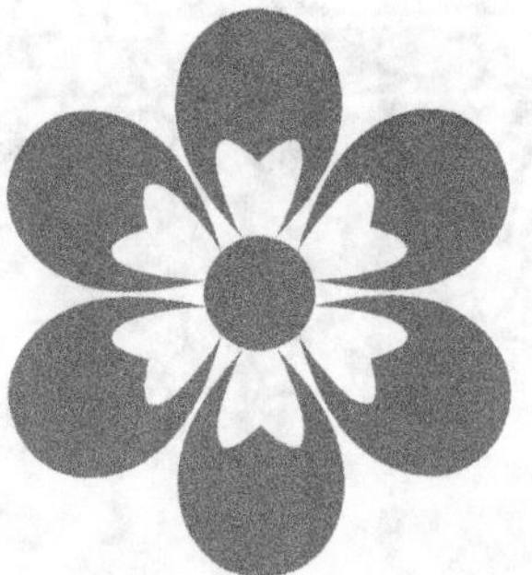

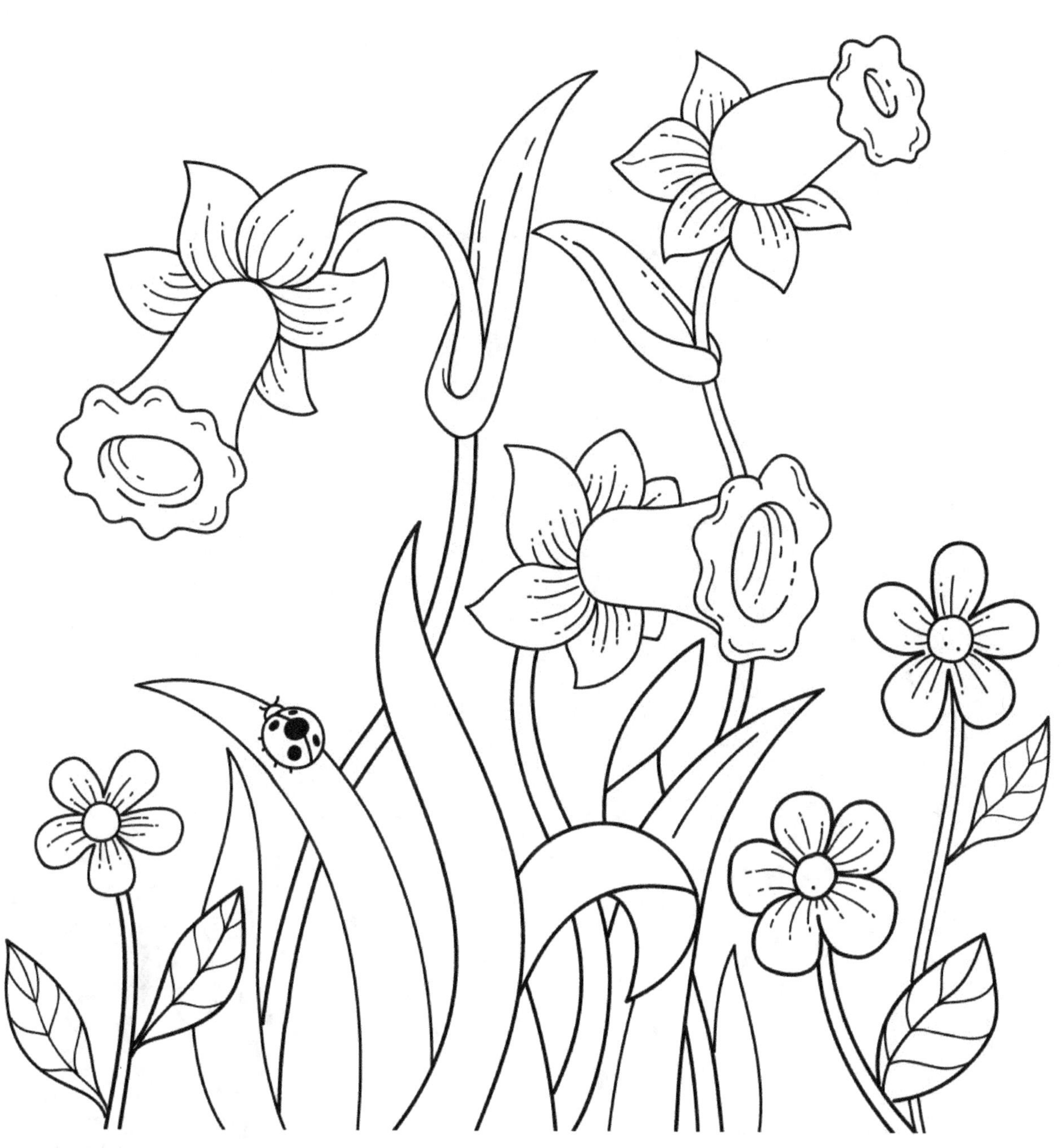

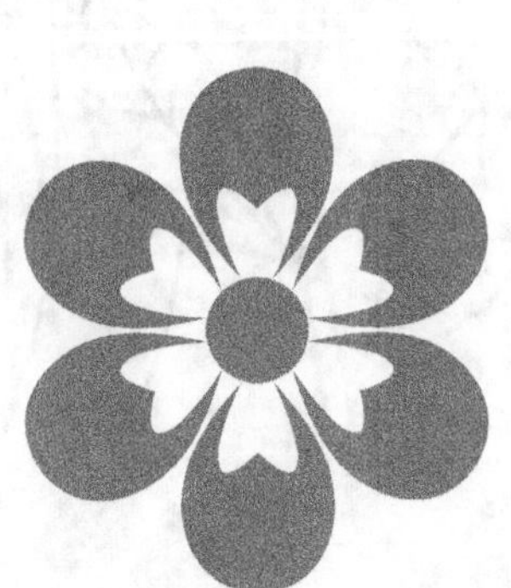

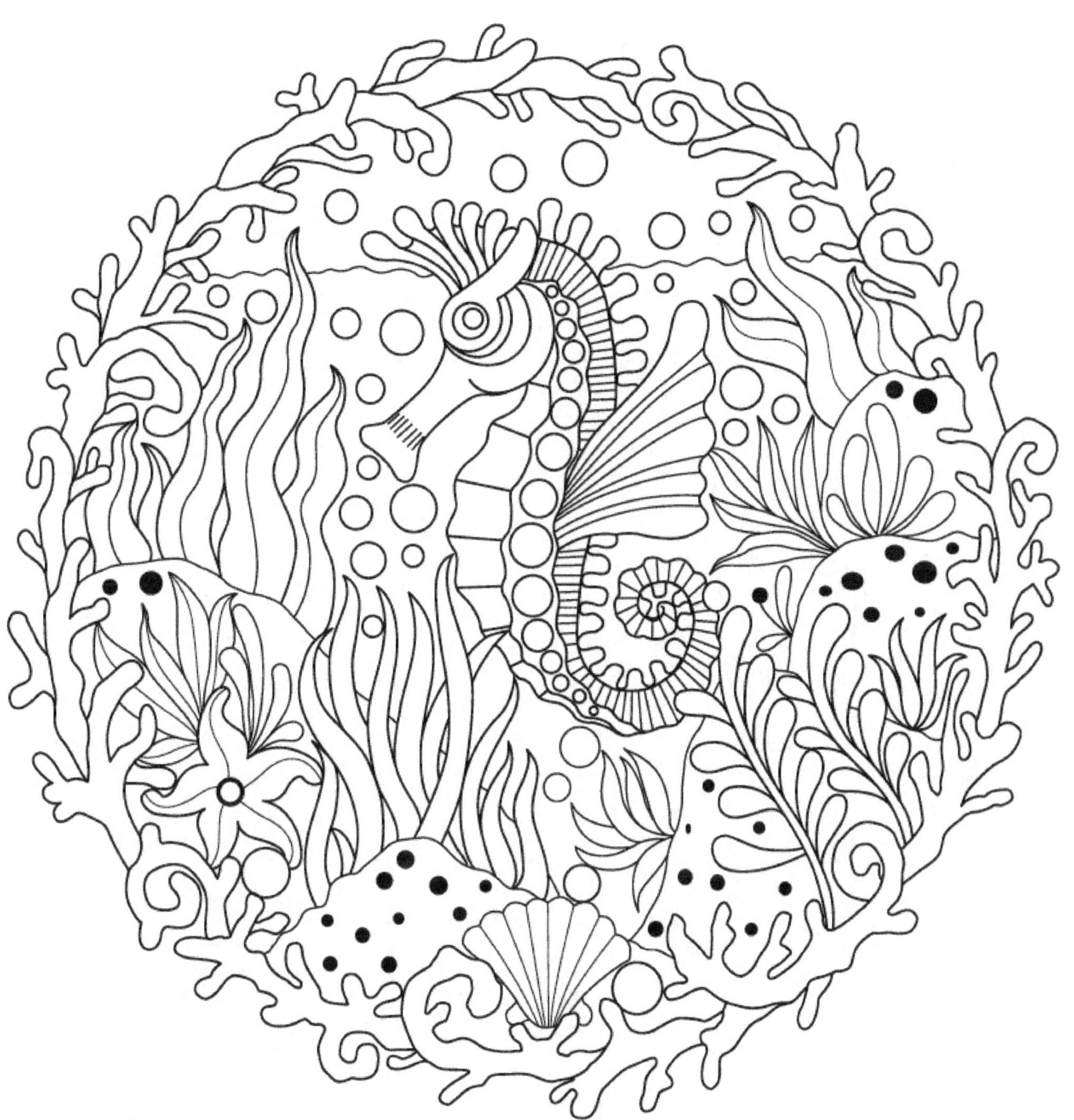

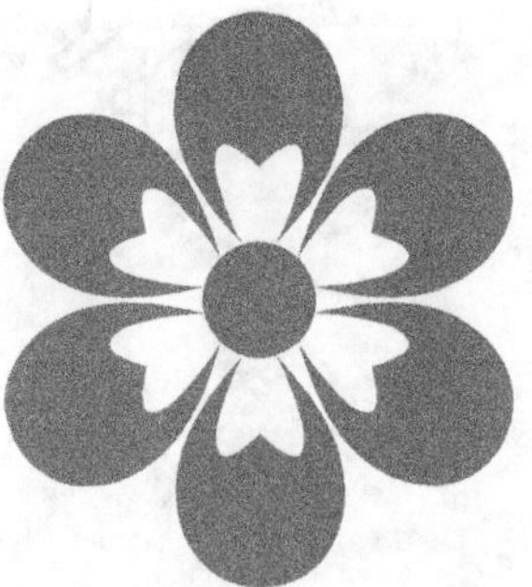

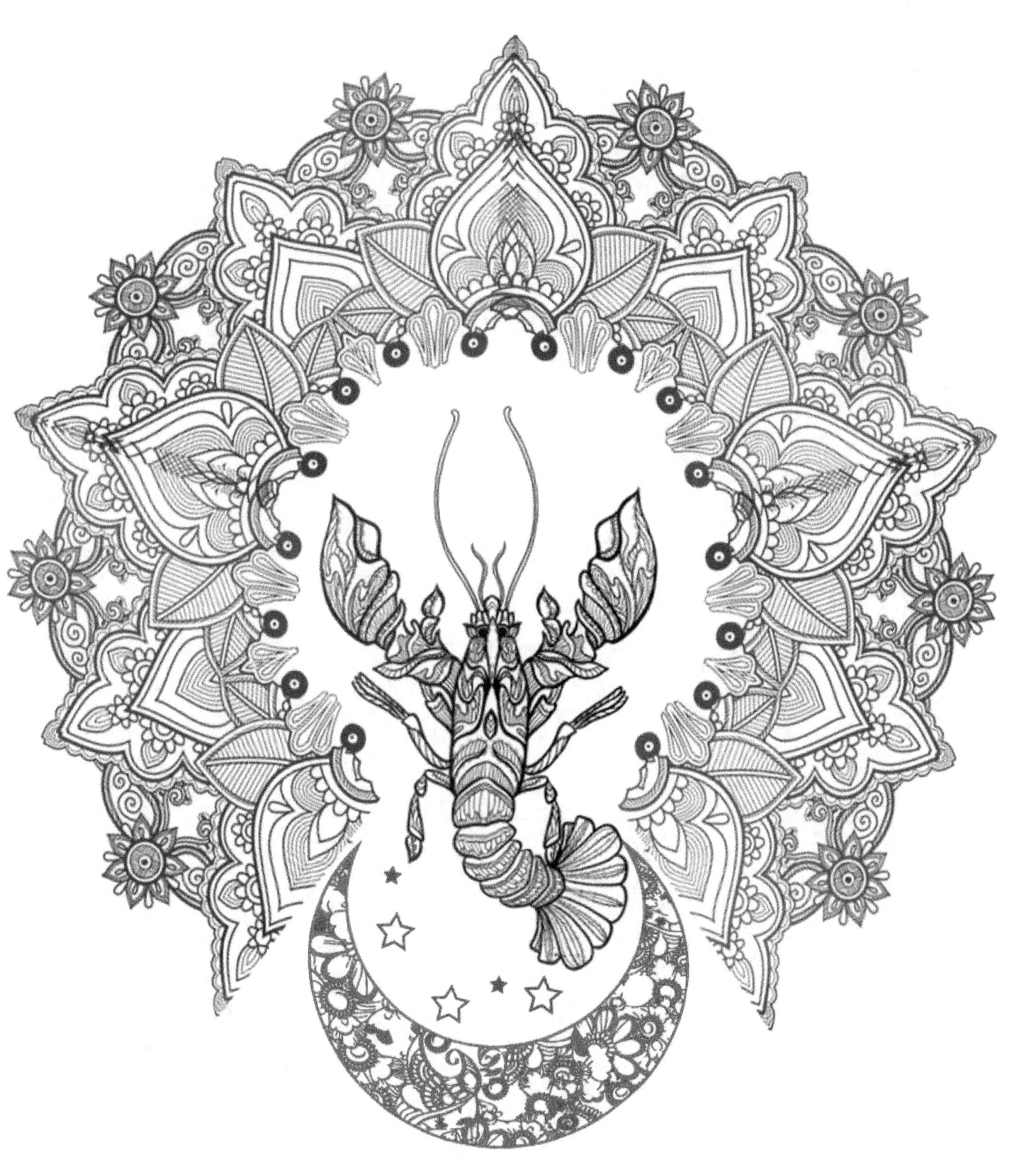

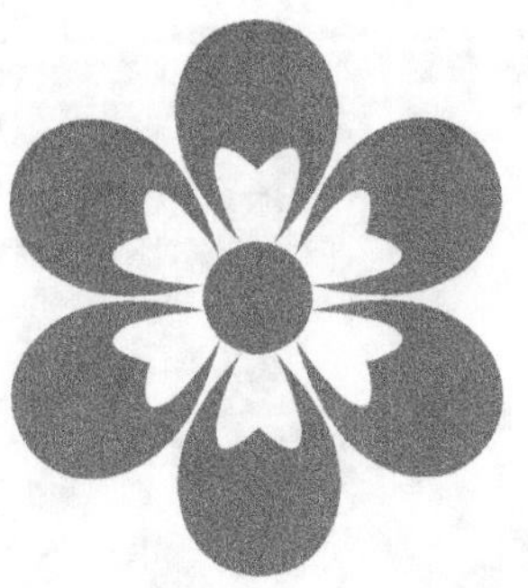

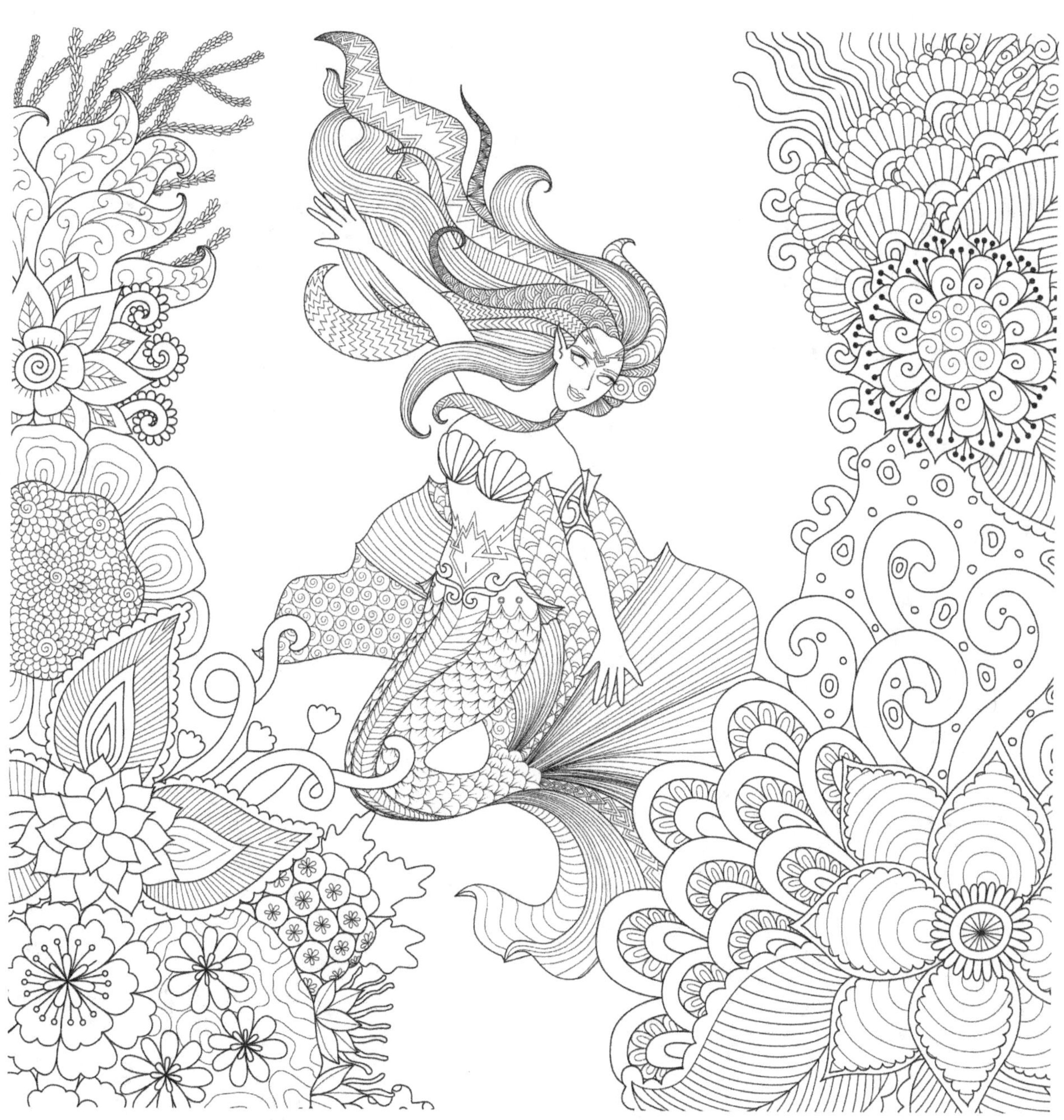

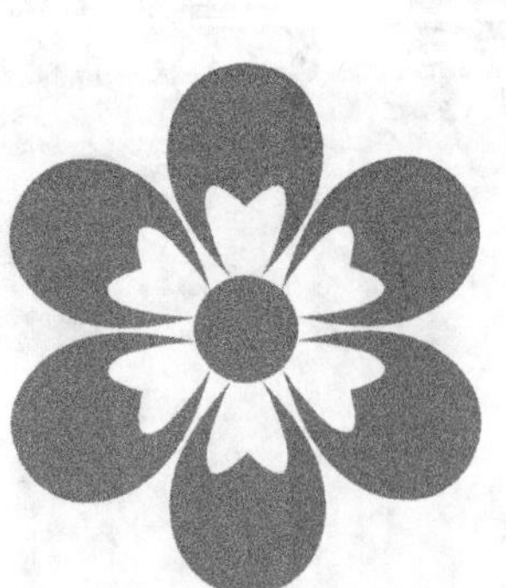

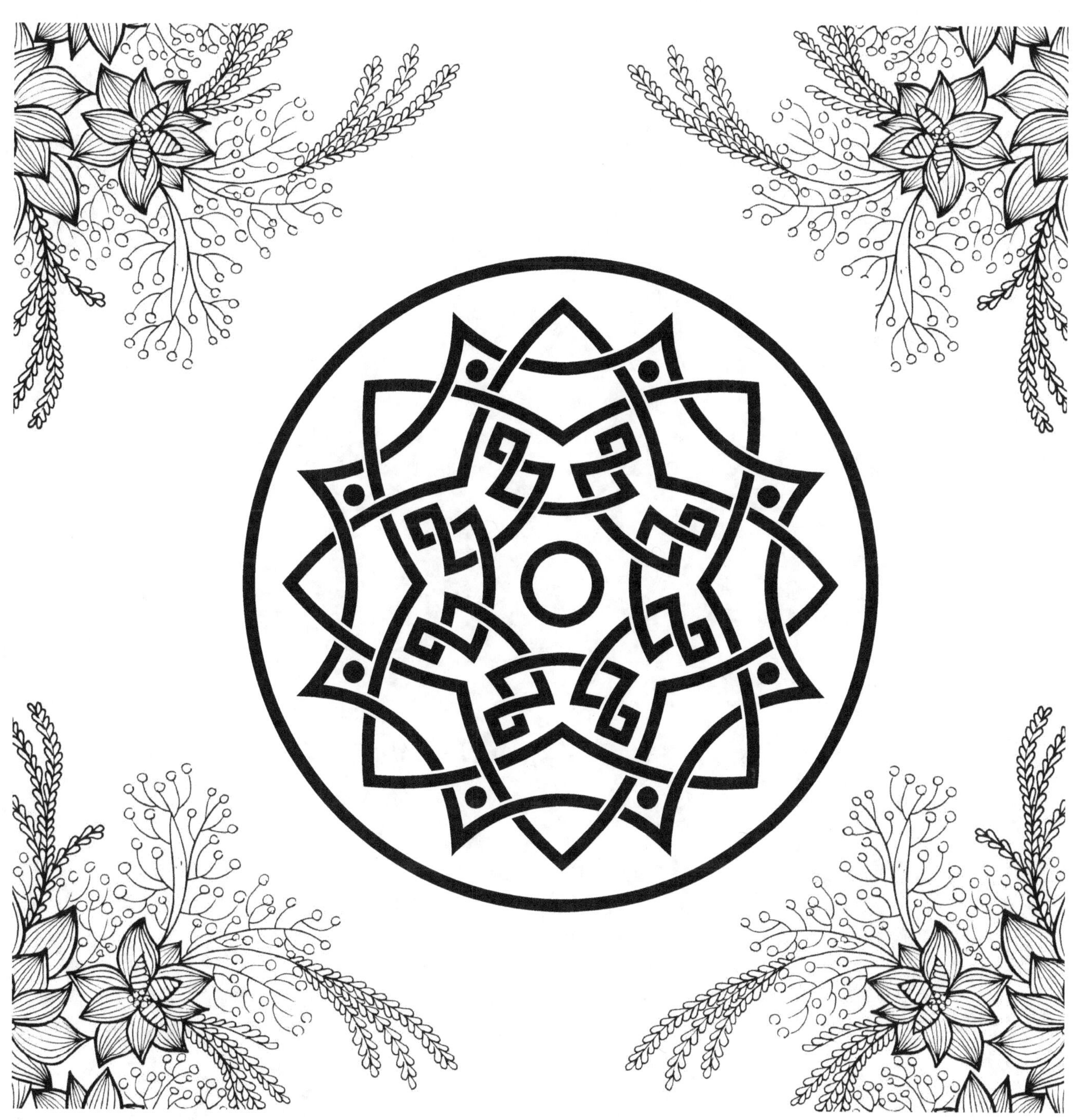

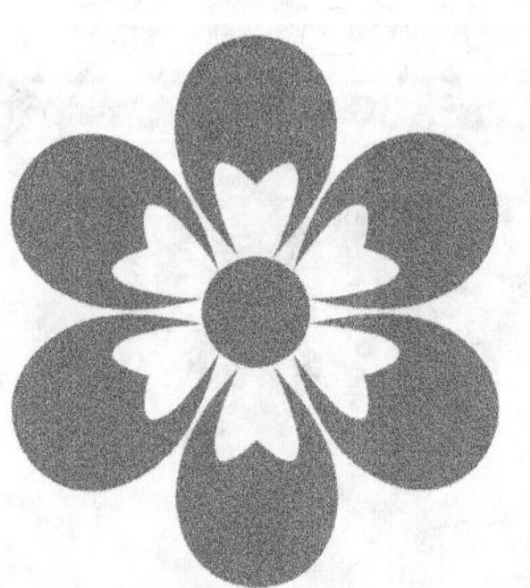

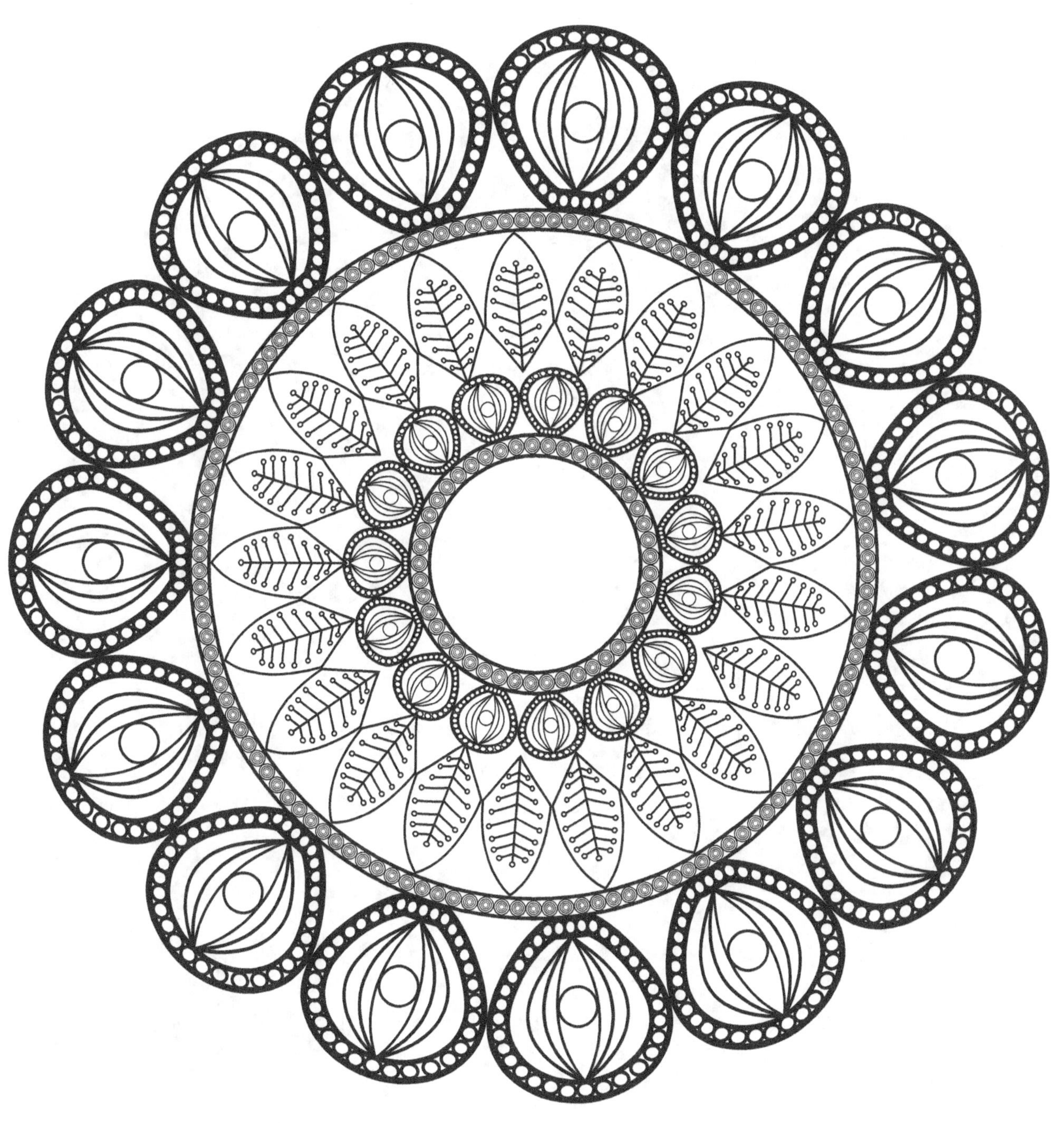

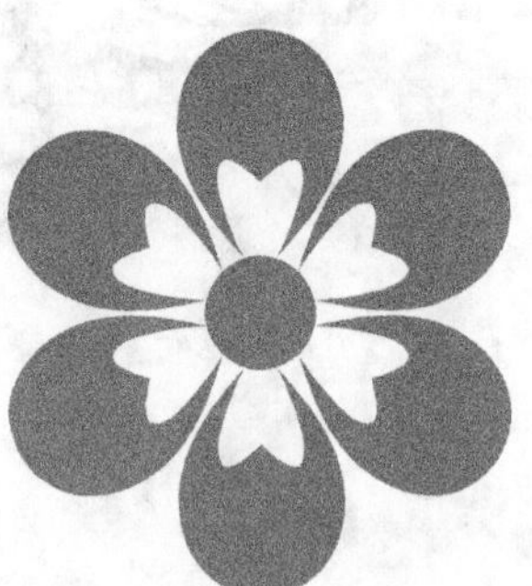

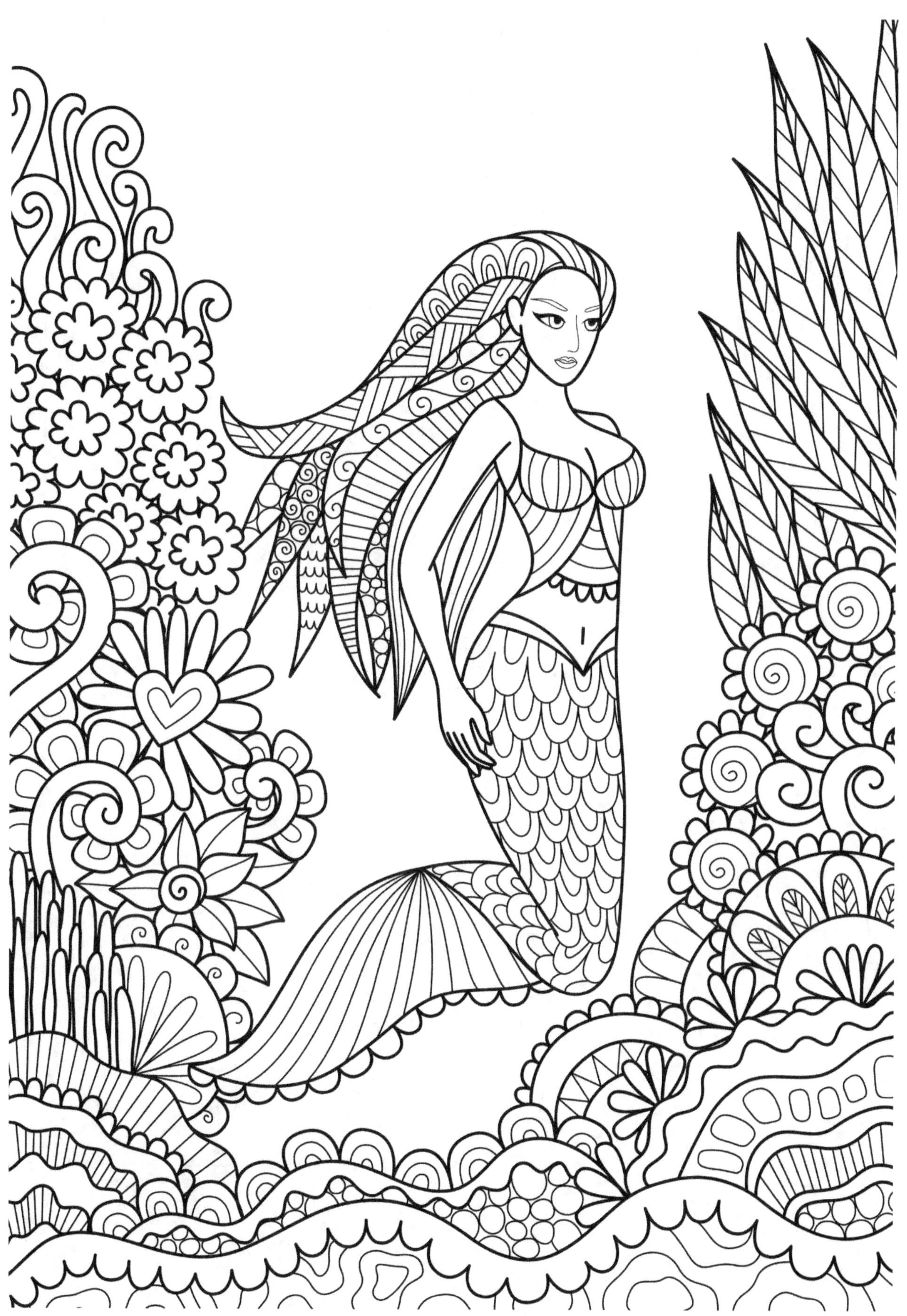

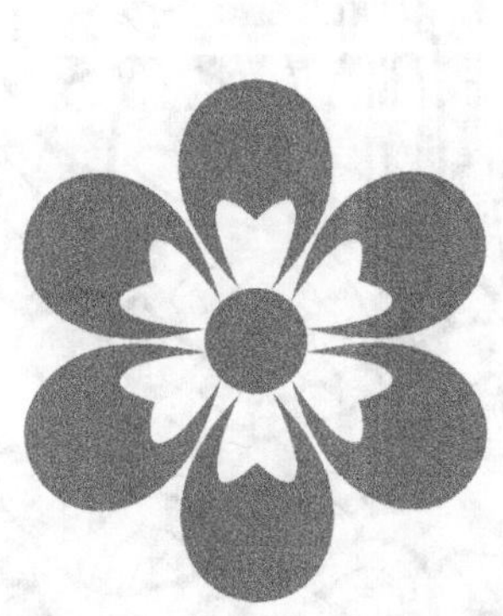

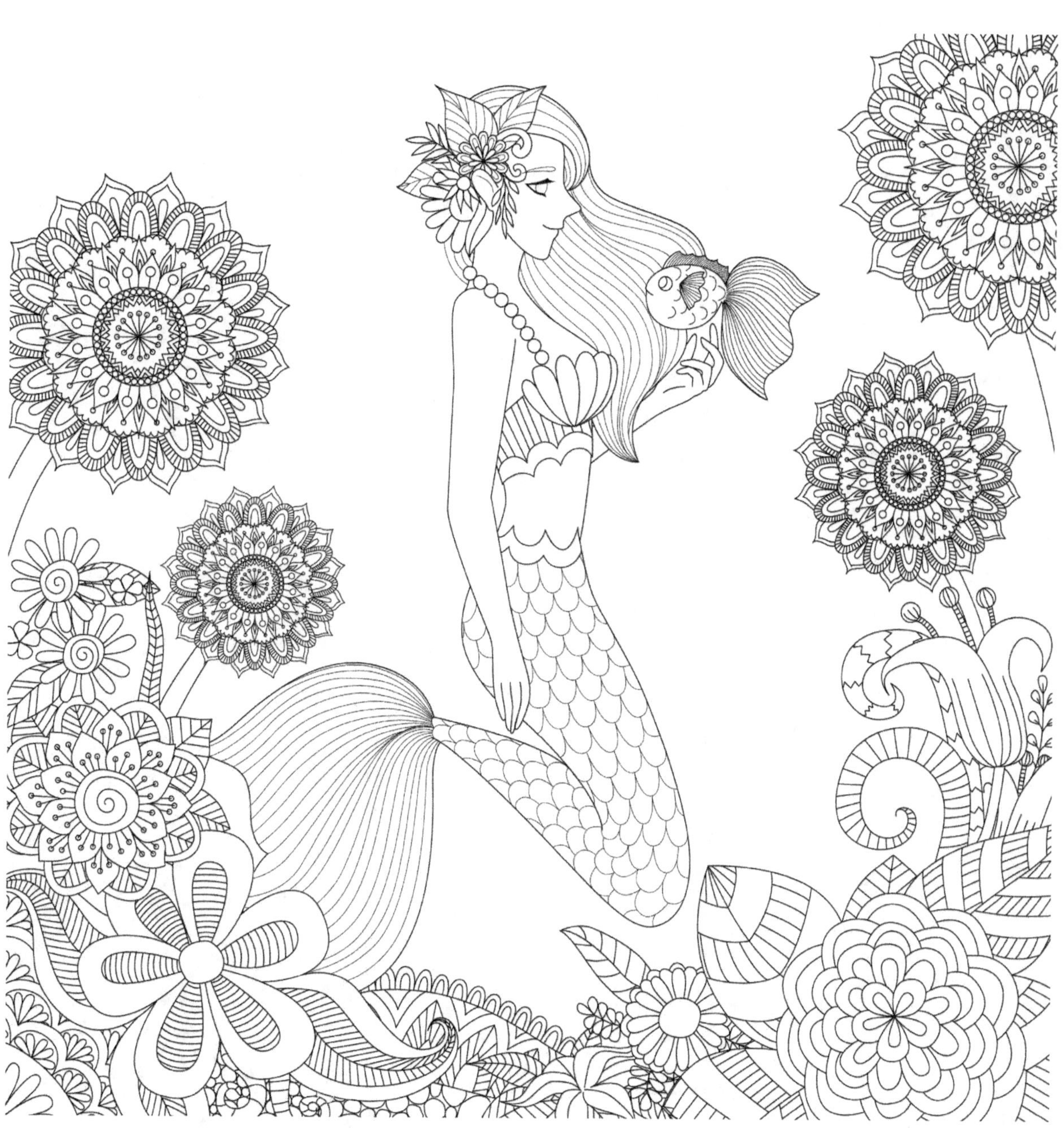

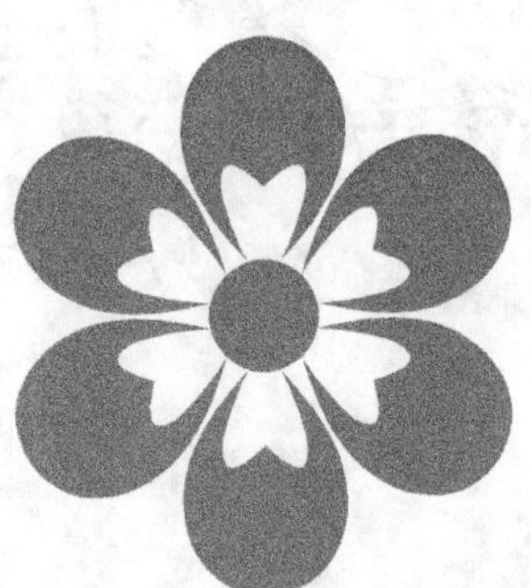

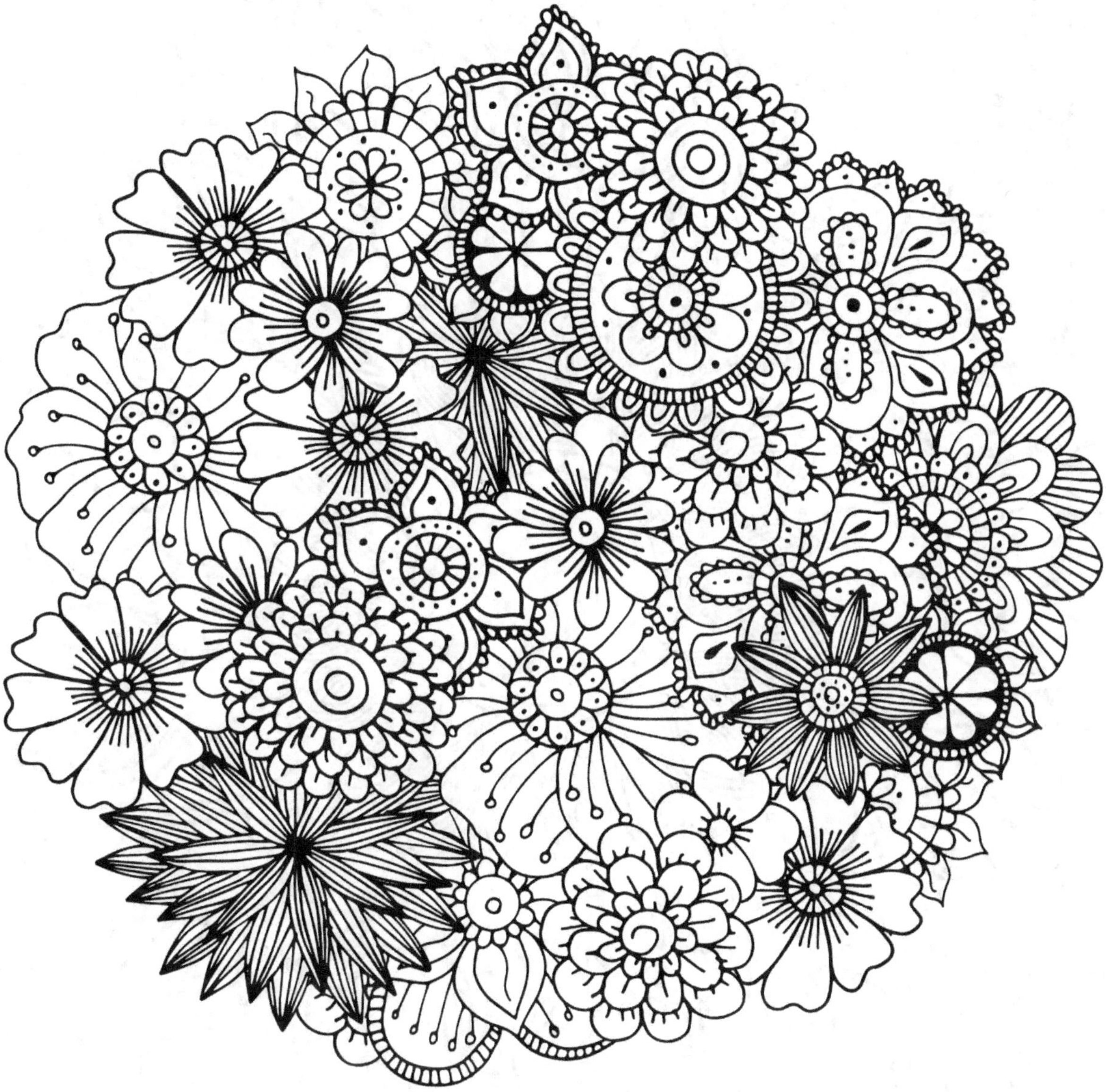

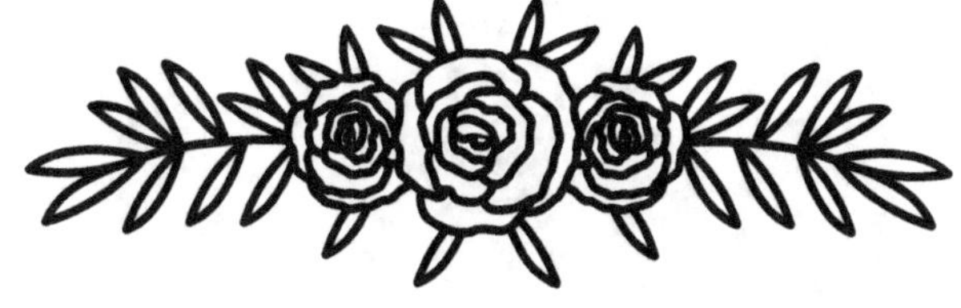

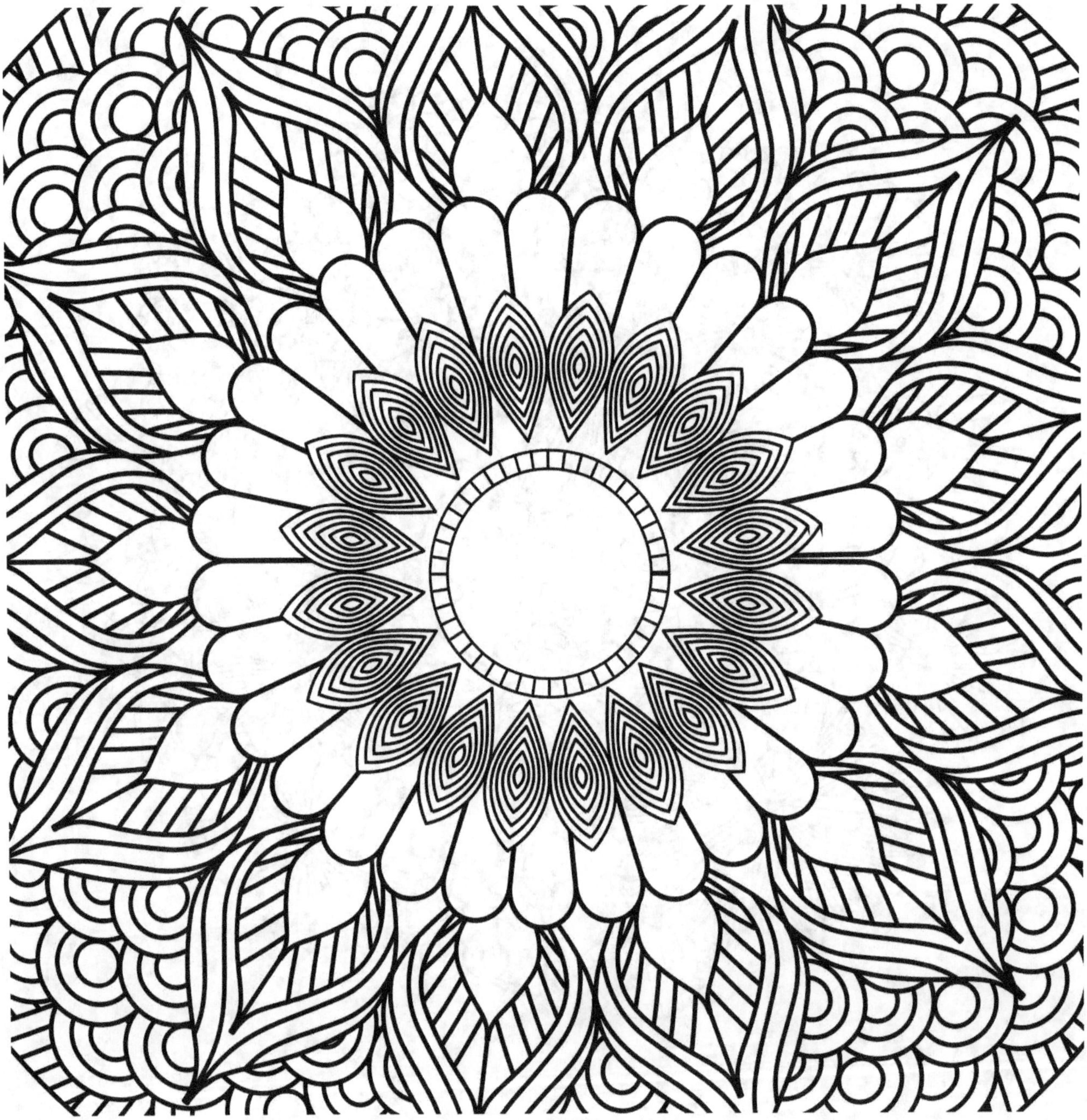

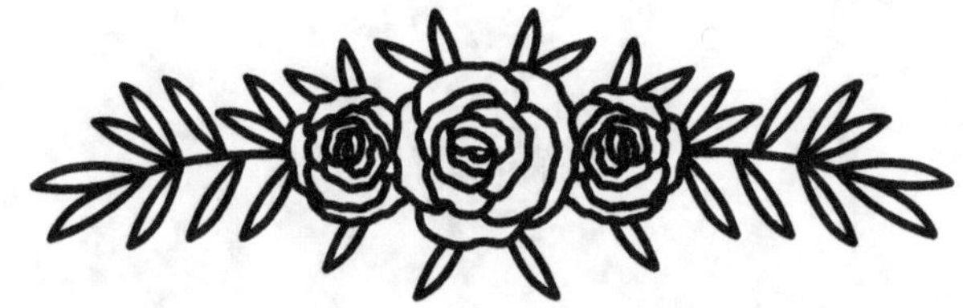

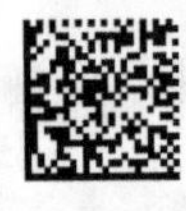

www.ingramcontent.com/pod-product-compliance
Lightning Source LLC
Chambersburg PA
CBHW080839160726

47999CB00009B/2955